Winners
and Losers

Winners and Losers
By Ron Chicone

Winners and Losers, by Ron Chicone
Copyright ©2014
ISBN: 978-0-9916067-2-6
Library of Congress Control Number: 2014915197

The main protagonists in this novel are fiction. Any similarity to persons living or dead is coincidental. Of the actual historical individuals mentioned, every effort had been made to keep their words, intentions, and actions consistent with recorded history.

No part of this publication may be reproduced or transmitted in any form or by any means, graphic, electronic, photocopy, recording, or by any information storage retrieval system—except for excerpts used for published review—without the written permission of the Author.

LA
Maison

Lamaisonpublishing.com
Vero Beach, Florida

Table of Contents

Acknowledgements vii
Exordium xi
Prologue xvii
John Nicholas Ringling 1
Adele Von Ohl Parker 32
Jekyll Island Club 47
Jesse Livermore 63
A Great American Institution 88
Originator of General Motors 112
One for the Road 157
Amelia Earhart 186
Vaudeville 240
The Cyclonic Lady of Vaudeville 244

Acknowledgements

As an author, when you solicit opinions from friends and colleagues, you are opening yourself up to a variety of criticisms, personal opinions and praise. Some people may like and admire you, others may just tolerate you, and of course, the same may be said vice-versa.

Various professions are represented among the personalities I have chosen to ask for counsel, and for the most part, I have been satisfied with their responses. They range from professors to biologists to telephone linemen.

The one person who had the most to do with the eventual outcome of this book is the editor, T. H. Pine, and he is responsible for all errors encompassing grammar, punctuation, etc., so all mistakes, errors and criticisms that you have about this book shall be laid at his feet and all praise directed entirely to me.

Without the help and encouragement of my long-term companion, Joan Lyons, who went over every word several times, ad nauseaum, I do not believe this endeavor would have been possible. So, in the line of succession on where to place the blame, Joan would be there.

Let's also remember that a publisher is involved in this deed, and as much as she would like to dodge any and all responsibility for the outcome, it's not going to happen. Her name is Janet Sierzant, the president of La Maison Publishing Company. Much hollering between her and I has occurred, though she would deny that fact. She would say that the hollering was all on my part, but don't believe her, she knows not what she says.

Finally, I would take note of persons who were involved, whether they knew it or not. Lisa Jeffra, Darla Myers and other denizens of the Indrio Road Gym, who I used indiscriminately for the polling of their knowledge in various aspects of long-ago times. When I requested if they had ever heard of vaudeville, in most cases a blank stare served as a response. Hell, I even encountered one sixteen year old teen who did not know who Frank Sinatra was! Oh, my God (or OMG! in the parlance of teens today!) Where did the years go?

Ms. Darla Myers was terribly involved in financial matters as pertains to the selection of securities on the Stock Market, all of which seemed to promptly descend when actually purchased, but, nevertheless, much discussion took place on the chapter of Jesse Livermore.

In Ms. Lisa Jeffra's case, she had experience in creative writing while attending college and gave valuable information on the form of my writing. She was nice enough not to give criticism that may have hurt my sensitive nature. So, when looking for a culprit, we could very possibly include her on the roster of blame.

Others at Nature's Way Gym, in central Fort Pierce, Florida, were very accommodating in our bull sessions, and of course, this took place while we were engaging in activities that provided great health benefits while we ensconced ourselves in very comfortable wicker chairs.

Let's see, there is Steve Stromak, now retired from the home moving business and he sees to it that his wife, Ruth, is still gainfully employed at the business while he and I solve the world's problems in those wicker chairs at the gym.

Mary Settle, the owner of the gym, has recently fallen in love and is still walking on a cloud. Well, live and learn.

A tip of the hat to Sue Horn, a former Burlesque Queen known as Camille the Cosmic Queen of Burlesque. Those were reckless, impulsive, exhilarating days which have left her with many sweet memories.

Lorain Hart, a teacher whose biggest joy is teaching children, may be the only one among us that has some degree of normalcy. Thanks

To Julie Jones, who proudly has the job of seeing to it that the gym has some amount of order to it, my thanks as well.

Lou Vadala says he's a bondsman, but you would be hard pressed to extrapolate the amount of time he is productively employed. His passion is Wall Street. Nevertheless he is a thoroughly enjoyable fellow to talk to.

Here at my abode, a condominium on the beach, I have many people to thank for their encouragement and support. Karen Downey, the Wise Old Owl, though old is just an expression; she is not really old. She is president of our association and has not buckled under the many obligations and duties that are inherent with being responsible for so many people.

Special mention must be made of Chuck and Lesa Kitzmiller, who are among the nicest and most charming couple I know. They were always standing ready with advice and inspiration.

To the Polka King and Queen, Joe and Chris Obara, the two people who love to dance as much as Joanie and I, although I would say with a touch more energy. We have spent many evenings with this lovely couple dancing the night away. Well, anyway up to nine p. m., at least.

Art and Judy Heon, very affable neighbors, have always been ready to give of their time to fix any problems that might arise. Art's background in engineering has been very helpful.

Bob Little and Rose Farley. I will never forget how Bob stood by me in my hour of greatest need. I call him Bob *Big*.

At the inauguration of my first book, Art and Julie Hughes were the first to order my last book, and even though a few errors occurred in the first edition, they enthusiastically recommended it to their friends.

Bela Berkes and Rose Ginolfi who had been a teacher, with an exponential, exceptional knowledge of grammar, made me a little uncomfortable when she read parts of my unedited work. Criticism is part and parcel of becoming, not only a better author but also a better person, but, damn! It's hard to improve on perfection.

Ron Chicone Jr. and his lovely wife, Lara, truly my biggest supporters and the man who stood by my bedside night after night, along with my companion of twenty-two years, Joan Lyons, while I, being the most belligerent S.O.B. in the hospital, fought for my life after a serious operation. The forbearance and loyalty he and she showed will stay with me for the rest of my life.

Accolades to all my friends, neighbors and others that I may have forgotten; thank you from the bottom of my Heart.

Ron Chicone

Exordium

Imagination is a requisite when reading this book, beginning with the following paragraph, a proliferation of words that is an ode to those people who can appreciate an application of diversity meant for those who live and think in another dimension.

Forward

An orgiastic, hedonistic, unreachable blend of guano that has no underpinning, no upside, no downside, no dreams, no field of honor, no higher calling, a life lived uneventfully, nothing to recommend to the ensuing generations, this would describe the forgotten people of this world.

They are not in this book.

The individuals who populate this missive are unique and will never be one of the postscripts to history. In their own way, they had a part to play. Yes, they were front and center in the making of the greatest country this old world has ever known, America.

They may become neglected but never forgotten. They were the capitalists that made our republic a success, a colossal success, far above our wildest dreams. Will this form of capitalism continue to exist?

Only a passage into eternity can give us an answer.

The Luminaries

John Ringling, for all time, will be known as the "Circus Man." He gave millions of people thrills and memories they will never forget. The high wire acts, elephants, tigers, clowns, cotton candy, and sawdust ... what would our life have been without the Big Top?

Adele Von Ohl, a grand dame of the first order, a pioneer if you will, gave us many memories of times past.

To those of you that are just attaining the age of majority, the Wild West and the Buffalo Bill Shows *really did* exist.

Jekyll Island Club. Go visit what, at one time, was the personification of a time in America called the "Gilded Age" which now languishes among the ghosts of a bygone era.

Billy Durant, a bon vivant, never was one to stop and smell the roses, not in the usual sense of the phrase. He *grew* the roses. He gave them their fragrance. He brought them to blooming maturity, thorns and all, and then went on to the next challenge.

Jessie Livermore lived for the game, the game of money, but not for fame or notoriety. He may have been the greatest stock trader that ever lived, loved by many, and hated by many more. To him money was just a way of keeping score, and when he lost the ability to make it, he ended his life in an ignoble fashion.

Horseracing is an American Institution. If you have ever watched the Kentucky Derby, listened to the strains of "My Old Kentucky Home," felt your heart beat in rhythm to the pounding of hooves coming down the stretch of Churchill Downs, all of this drowned out by the roar of over 150,000 fans, then you would know the magic of the "Sport of Kings."

One for the Road is the story of a quintessential woman who went through adversity and a failed marriage and made an exciting and successful life for herself. You say you don't know her? Oh yes you do! She may be your neighbor, your sister, your cousin, maybe even *you*. After all what is success? Is it not what we all want, we call it "happiness?"

Amelia Earhart, lived one of the most daunting lives of all, the antithesis of uninspiring. With this one soaring woman, you have the embodiment of a spirit and flame that cannot be doused … a life lived to the fullest.

Eva Tanguay, a powerful star of a theatrical time in America called vaudeville, was a puzzle that lived within an enigma. She grabbed at life with an exuberance that could not be denied, a flame that burst into stars, in an extravaganza of colors and finally perished, still fantasizing about greatness to come.

This book is a narrative of legends that in most cases no longer survive, except in the pages of tomes written by authors like me. In our world, we brought them to life in the corridors of our minds and walked side by side with each one of them, through the amorphous vapors of time.

ROCK ME TO SLEEP

Elizabeth Akers Allen 1832-1911

Backward, turn backward, O Time, in your flight,
Make me a child again just for to-night!
Mother, come back from the echoless shore,
Take me again to your heart as of yore;
Kiss from my forehead the furrows of care,
Smooth the few silver threads out of my hair;
Over my slumbers your loving watch keep;—
Rock me to sleep, mother,—rock me to sleep!

Backward, flow backward, O tide of the years!
I am so weary of toil and of tears,—
Toil without recompense, tears all in vain,—
Take them, and give me my childhood again!
I have grown weary of dust and decay,—
Weary of flinging my soul-wealth away;
Weary of sowing for others to reap;—
Rock me to sleep, mother,—rock me to sleep!

Tired of the hollow, the base, the untrue,
Mother, O mother, my heart calls for you!
Many a summer the grass has grown green,
Blossomed and faded our faces between:
Yet, with strong yearning and passionate pain,
Long I to-night for your presence again.
Come from the silence so long and so deep;—
Rock me to sleep, mother,—rock me to sleep!

Over my heart, in the days that are flown,
No love like mother-love ever has shone;
No other worship abides and endures,—

Faithful, unselfish, and patient like yours:
None like a mother can charm away pain
From the sick soul and the world-weary brain.
Slumber's soft calms o'er my heavy lids creep;—
Rock me to sleep, mother,—rock me to sleep!

Come, let your brown hair, just lighted with gold,
Fall on your shoulders again as of old;
Let it drop over my forehead to-night,
Shading my faint eyes away from the light;
For with its sunny-edged shadows once more
Happily will throng the sweet visions of yore;
Lovingly, softly, its bright billows sweep;—
Rock me to sleep, mother,—rock me to sleep!

Mother, dear mother, the years have been long
Since I last listened your lullaby song:
Sing, then, and unto my soul it shall seem
Womanhood's years have been only a dream.
Clasped to your heart in a loving embrace,
With your light lashes just sweeping my face,
Never hereafter to wake or to weep;—
Rock me to sleep, mother,—rock me to sleep!

Love, the one constant that can never be lost through the ravages of time.

A salute to those in the Arena
Not the spectators
You cannot win unless you play the game

Prologue

"Winning is the only thing," said famed football coach Vince Lombardi. It follows that Mr. Lombardi had his share of losing before he became a winner. I believe losing is the catalyst that brings together the strength of character I know is a latent inherency in everyone.

I have always been fascinated by people who were once winners, and then, because of life's circumstances, became losers or those who started with every possible disadvantage and ended with great wealth and a legacy rich in legendary lessons learned from their days spent in the arena of life. These were the doers and not the spectators. In this book, I will explore what made them winners and losers.

I believe, from my unique vantage point—having spent over thirty years as a registered investment adviser—that my experience with the various, fascinating people I have met, and had close personal, and sometimes fleeting relationships with, has taught me a valuable lesson; everyone in one way or another is a winner and loser. I am surrounded by people who have a story to tell, and have tales of great heroism, victories, and abject losing.

My youth became my albatross. Inattention and naiveté abounded in my youthful years, so it became my loss that these jewels were never afforded the attention they so richly deserved. I believe most of us have an eagerness to tell our own story, and never truly listen to what others have to say. Do you really know your neighbor, or the people you regularly socialize with? I am betting the things they could tell you would give a new awareness of who they are.

I believe everybody thinks a book could be written on their lives, and yes, even you, the reader probably have great stories to tell. In this book, I will be more concerned with fascinating individuals that had an effect on our lives in one way or another. I made an exception in one case and included an exquisite, majestic, ghostly club, more alive in its own way, than any individual I have known, I also highlighted others, who, in some way, were instrumental in the history of the world, or our country, except in a few instances of people I have known personally, who never were well known, aside from their limited circle. They became figures of great personal interest to me. It is my hope that, in some way, their experiences will be of value to you the reader. The tales I will render in this missive are important, at least to me, and hopefully, you. Some of these tales have been lost for the most part to the mists of time.

A question I have asked of many people is an improbable one, but one which should be known by the majority of the population in this country and the world. Yet, not one in twenty could give me the answer to this question. At one time, and at least until the last few years, the largest corporation the world has ever known was a company formed and headquartered in Michigan by a salesman of horse carts. Do you know this man? *I thought not.* The answer to this will be revealed in the latter portion of this book,

In doing research for this manuscript, and in the search for personages I may include, brought me to an acquaintance I had known just a few years before her death in 1969. I knew she had great stories to tell, but I was young, foolish, busy, and did not listen. Oh how I wish I could go back in time and have her tell me about her life.

These are some of her experiences and accomplishments:

- One of the highest paid actresses in New York, on Broadway, in the early 1900's.
- A highly skilled equestrian.
- Rode with the Buffalo Bill Wild West show as a featured trick rider and a stuntman in the early days of Hollywood. It would be a misnomer to say stuntwoman

- because the stunts she performed were for the leading male cowboys of the era.
- ➤ She may have been married to Butch Cassidy, the infamous outlaw. I will outline the coincidences I have encountered in her life as pertains to this relationship.

It will be up to you to consider the things creating an aura of intriguing mystery about her life; this should be of great interest to all readers, I'm sure much controversy will ensue. Can you imagine the things I could ask if she could be brought back, and I, now in my heightened state of wisdom, which age and life's experience brings on, could talk, not only about the things she had done, but also her feelings while in the throes of success, in failures that occurred, in loves she had and people she had intimate contact with, Bill Cody, Annie Oakley, Bat Masterson, and myriad other legendary things she could tell, now loss to the ages. Even now I feel a pain in my heart and a little mist in my eye's just thinking about the lost opportunity's I had encountered along the way. Because like so many young men I was full of passion and in a hurry to get to the rainbow's end. I did not realize this dichotomy.

As a young man I was standing on the epicenter of the rainbow and to go forward meant going to the portal of old age, which brings with it declining passion and ambition and those diminishing, but much sought after dreams. The pot of gold was at the center of the rainbow, not the end.
All I had to do was look up, and there it was.

In some areas of this book, I may use literary license and it will be what I believe had actually happened, so, be that as it may, please bear with me. It's true many of us had inappropriate or, may I say, *all* of us had lost loves, anger, disillusionment, embarrassment and bad choices concerning spouses and careers. We had, many times, feelings of deep depression, and yet, there were times of wonderful fulfillment and successes which made us feel as Mark Antony felt when he rode at the head of his Roman Legions after a successful campaign. He rode to the cheers and the bands and the pageantry of his countrymen.

Some of us have met with wild success and others with more than a modicum of satisfaction, but all of us have many, many *REGRETS*.

Considering the hard-earned successes, disappointments, and embarrassing moments I have experienced in the past, if I were asked, would I do it again, you can bet I would gladly do it all over again. That always reminds me of part of a poignant poem I will paraphrase: Pause, o pause, time in thy flight; make me a boy again, just for tonight.

One chapter in this book will be one that concerns a part of my life. It has to do with gambling and bookmaking as it applies to the racetrack. I have drawn on my experience as one that has lost a coin or two at the track. If you want to enjoy a microcosm of an exciting life with all of its joys, sorrows, highs and lows, it can be found at the racetrack, not only at the betting windows, or the seats, where can be found on the floor crumpled up losing betting tickets that were once held tightly in hopeful hands. Also, the backstretch where the barns and sleeping quarters of the people who live and die with this great American institution are contained. Certainly, I knew what it was like to have lost the rent money and trying to explain it to my wife. I always remember what Mickey Rooney had to say about the races. The first time he went he lost five dollars and then spent $100,000 trying to get that five dollars back.

It has been my privilege to know and been friends with two people who will be an integral part of that particular chapter. One, a well-known jockey and trainer, another a longtime trainer at a prominent race track. All of these friends have amazing stories to tell and I have certainly enjoyed hearing them as I hope you will be.

When expounding on Winners and Losers, how can we forget some of the greatest stock market plungers of our time? Who now remembers Bernard Baruch? In 1910, he was known as the Lone Wolf of Wall Street and became a valued advisor to presidents. Or Jesse Livermore, who became known as the boy plunger, and the hated Great Bear of Wall Street?

As an axiom concerning Wall Street, one which meant much to me. *The street begins in a cemetery (Trinity Church Cemetery) and ends in a river (the Hudson River).* Our country went through one of the greatest cataclysmic boom and bust eras in our history. Specifically, in the '20s and '30s, this led us into a different system of government, which relied more heavily on the interference of governing bodies into our economy and personal lives. Whether a good thing or not, it is pervious to my central theme, and as a matter of fact, is still being batted about today and I imagine will go on indefinitely in the future.

The 1800s and the early 1900s, '20s, and '30s, has to be described as an era that made legends out of people, such as the DuPonts, Melons, Rockefellers, Pulitzers and a host of other well-known millionaires we thought of as Robber Barons.

In this book, I will take you to a little known place, a club as it were, that was a winner and loser, so exclusive, only the titans of industry could belong, a place so isolated (and still is) only the fortunate few know of its existence, and yes, even you can stay there now. This particular place sent chills up my spine as I sat in the spectacular turn-of-the-century dining room and realized I was among the ghosts of the giants of a bygone age that I had only read about. In their own way, they were the trailblazers, creating the greatest country the world has ever known.

This book has truly been a labor of love. In most cases, the people, places and events, I herein pontificate on, I did not personally know. Spiritually, they were with me in my dreams and flights of fantasy and of adventure. For me, as a youngster, the library was a wonderland filled with escapades, adventure, and voyages to faraway lands filled with close friends. At least, to me, they were as real as other things we cannot see, but we could feel; wind, warmth, cold, the magic of the night, the impending sunrise, and scents that still trigger emotional tugs on my heart. I want to fill this book with these friends, so, you see, this volume is really revisiting old acquaintances. I am now starting down the last mile of my existence. Many of the people that, to me, were larger than life, are now gone or have faded into just caricatures of themselves. I would love to bring them back just one more time.

Oh, where did they go?

A place where I will soon follow, but, for now, I will search the corridors of my mind, and through the magic of words, bring them back for just a little while.

Ron Chicone

John Nicholas Ringling
Maestro of Greatest Show on Earth

The Impresario

Ca' d'Zan

Ringling Family

The Rolls Royce came to a smooth stop in front of the rear entrance of Madison Square Garden, where the offices were located. A chauffer moved, just as smoothly, to the rear door of the imposing automobile. A male figure, of stately presence and a commanding air, slowly unwound from the back seat, and with alacrity, attained his full height. With a touch of his fingers to the brim of his homburg, he dismissed his chauffer. Striding purposefully to the entrance of this recently built structure, he looked side to side and up and down, drinking in all the many details of this building. It was a paean to his enormous input in the completion of this rambling edifice.

The man standing here was none other than John Nicholas Ringling and this building, now being run by Tex Rickard, was built with the specifications of the Ringling Circus in mind. Yes, he was the ringmaster of the Greatest Show on Earth, a circus not matched in its veracity and unequaled enormity. Bringing this colossus to the millions of fans around the world was this man's mission in life. He, along with his brothers, built this entertainment juggernaut from the ground up starting as the entertainment themselves and gradually growing until all of the brothers became possessors of multiple millions.

John's first act was as a clown. This man would later prove to be anything but a clown. His bearing and style, in which he conducted himself, cried out for officiousness. The manner he used when issuing orders was brusque, his way of indicating he was in a preeminent position.

Making his way into the cavernous arena, pleasing sounds met his senses, sounds made by workmen who were setting up the various apparatuses to be used by the Greatest Show on Earth. Approaching a supervising workman, he held out his hand.

"Louis I am glad to have run into you at this time," he said softly.

Louis was rather surprised to see John there that early. Generally, the boss would not show up prematurely, while Lou was in the early stages of his effort to get the garden ready for the circus. He impudently turned to John, and said facetiously, "For God sakes, what the hell are you doing here?"

"Louis, bear with me for a moment. There has been a recurring thought in my mind I need to address. You know, many times I can be clairvoyant. I know you have heard this before and feel I am being foolish, but, dammit Louis, do not laugh." John said this with a twinkle in his eye. It was evident John and Louis were good friends.

"What the crap are you worrying about now John?"

This repartee was common between John and his workers, at least those who had been with him for a while. They dearly loved him and knew his bark was worse than his bite. In fact, he wanted this type of dialogue between his employees and himself. This fostered a relaxed atmosphere, and along with his fairness in wages paid and the honesty he displayed—rare in the business—gave him an unparalleled degree of loyalty from his associates.

"Listen Louis, I am very serious about this. I have just signed a new high wire act from Germany. When we open, they will be the featured performers, center ring. I have a strong intuition there may be a malfunction in one of the trapezes, cables, or the platforms. Until further notice, they will perform with nets."

Louis looked at John's rather round face, seeing the seriousness that he exhibited. "John you can bet I will check and double check every wire, swing, platform, and anything else I can think of," he said, reaching out to his boss.

"I knew I could depend on you. I have every confidence that your performance, as always, will be exemplary."

Louis went on to say, the only problem I see, "Is the disappointment of the spectators when the troupe performs with nets."

"Believe me Louis; they would be more disappointed if a lifeless body was carried out of the arena. Lou, I'll talk to you later. Give me a shout if you need anything."

With that, John turned and headed for the elevator. As he arrived at the floor where conferences were held, he heard men bantering with each other. With anticipation he opened and stepped through the giant oak doors of the conference room. Tex Rickard and Dwight Baum looked up amid a stridency of conversation between them. Both had awaited the arrival of

Ringling. Here he was, somehow larger than life, and these men were true friends, their ascendency in the world of business depended on each other. John, who had a controlling interest in the Garden, was especially important, but the success of his main enterprise depended on the performance of the other two. The excitement of seeing each other was evident.

Tex was unabashedly a rising leader in the sports field and would lead Madison Square Garden to become the epitome of all that was important in the field of athletics, sporting events, games and other diversions, only equaled by past glories and debauchery of the Coliseum in Rome. Dwight, on the other hand, was the architect of Ringling's new ostentatious home being built in Sarasota, Florida. Dubbed the last mansion of the Gilded Age, the manse was so unique and different, Baum was fearful his peers may cast aspersions on his abilities. With that in mind, he never mentioned Ringling's home named Ca' d'Zan—which in Venetian dialect interpreted as *House of John*—in any of his future resumes. Dwight was once an associate of the firm of McKim, Mead, and White, headed by a genius who was more of an artist than an architect.

Stanford White   **Evelyn Nesbit Thaw**   **Harry Thaw**

Mr. Baum learned his craft at the knee of Stanford White, the guiding light of homes and buildings that had become icons of the very best money could buy. Stanford White owned this enterprise, and led his team of architects who erected and built imposing homes and commercial structures in America. The most revered and esteemed families had some contact with Mr. White. The names that littered the coffers of McKim, Mead, and White rang with the sound of extreme wealth, Villard, Whitney, Vanderbilt, Pulitzer, and many others, not to mention the second Madison Square Garden and other buildings of note.

∞∂∞

Stanford White was implicated in one of the most celebrated murder cases of its day. The year was 1906. Evelyn Nesbit, a chorus girl and model, had a dalliance with Stanford. It seems he loved young chorus girls and would entice them to his domicile containing a red velvet swing, where they would be entertained much to his delight. Evelyn married a well-off gentleman named Harry Thaw, who had serious mental problems and resented Stanford's relations with his wife before their marriage. He took it upon himself to shoot Mr. White three times in the face while attending a play on the rooftop of Madison Square Garden. Unbelievably, a jury acquitted him of this murder. He used an insanity plea, the first in the history of jurisprudence. This terrible incident was enshrined in two books and movies; *The Red Velvet Swing* and *Ragtime*.

∞∂∞

Ringling sauntered into this meeting room—seemingly more like a sumptuous chamber in an exclusive men's club—and heavily heaved himself into a plush soft chair, allowing the tiredness he felt from his recent travels to wash over him. He had hurried to get to New York to be with his lovely wife, Mabel. He had been visiting several areas, arranging for the circus to visit cities worthy of the Greatest Show on Earth. (What he meant by worthy; was a metropolis prosperous enough to guarantee a lively turn out for the show?) This was the causative agent depleting his energies and now, sitting there, the inner glow and satisfaction he felt was for a job well done.

Reaching into the inner pocket of his overcoat, John exposed a bottle of well-aged rye whiskey. In the years of prohibition, one had to be careful. On this occasion there was a small cheer when he exhibited the bottle. Glasses were not needed as the bottle was passed around the room. The conversation centered on Tex Richard as he expounded on the upcoming fights he was currently promoting for the Garden.

Tex Richard boxing promoter   **Tiger Flowers and Harry Greb**

"Tex, what do you have on the calendar for the next promotion here at the Garden?" Dwight said.

"This next fight, coming in a few months, will knock your goddam hat off, Dwight. Harry Greb, who has recently lost his championship belt, is going to make a comeback fighting Tiger Flowers."

"Excuse me Tex, don't you think Greb may be a little over the hill?" John asked.

"Listen to me John; you better fuckin' believe I'm worried. It's not so much he's over the hill, but, when I was watching his last fight, it seemed to me he was hit with too many telegraphed punches he never saw coming. It makes me think something is wrong with his eyes."

"Tex, if I was you, I'd be damned careful you aren't the one to promote a fight that gets a man blinded," John said.

"Thank you for your concern. This fight was one I had to make for the Garden. Any time you are promoting fights, risks are the nature of the business. Unfortunately, it is incumbent on me to consider the number of asses I can seat in this place every week." *(Harry Greb loss to Tiger Flowers. Entered the fight blind in one eye and never fought again)*

"If at all possible, my ass will be one of the spectators," John responded. Getting the attention of Baum, he said, "Dwight, I'm sorry I have to tell you this, but changes are going to be made in Ca' d'Zan. My supply of capital is not without some limits, so here is what I propose we do. I hope you concur with me on these changes.

Ringling continued conversing with Dwight and informing him the total size of the home he was building in Sarasota, Florida, would have to decrease. He needed to draw up new plans and give them to the builder, Owen Burns, before he went too far with the construction phase. This caused an amount of consternation for Baum, who was used to ignoring costs because of the massive amount of wealth his usual clients possessed. He considered his reputation to be put upon if he produced a product not worthy of his talent. However, over many years, John and Baum had become great friends and now that friendship was being tested.

In the glow of the rye whiskey, they worked out the details they were committing to, and decided to get together at Baum's offices, with his assistants present and the acquiescence of Mable, who would be the driving force on any plans concerning the interior of the home. Thus, the plans would be updated.

Mable was adamant about what she wanted on the core of the home and many times superseded Baum's superior knowledge. In actuality, this apparent overbearingness on the part of Mable worked to make this home an outstanding example of Venetian architecture, yet accommodating the surroundings and weather of Florida.

This meeting of friends continued with a great amount of joviality, reminiscences, and ribald jokes, until late into the evening. John, feeling a little ashamed of himself coming home so late to Mable, plus more than a small amount in his cups—meaning a little inebriated—pulled together, and said a hearty goodbye to his cohorts and was off, traveling the short distance to his home on Fifth Avenue.

The Ringling Obsession

John and Mable spent a considerable amount of time in Europe gathering the things that would be their legacy to the world. Art became an obsession, consuming an ever-increasing allotment of their life. Italy held an enormous, amorous allure, especially the architecture of the buildings and grand homes of the aristocrats.

Samson and Delilah by
Peter Paul Rubens

Sistine Chapel
Michelangelo

The Baroque paintings of the old masters, held a fascination never to be satisfied. John thirsted for the great masterpieces of Paolo Veronese, Alvero du Piero, Govanni Antonio Gasolo, and Michelangelo. What would become the centerpiece of his future enormous collection, would be located at a museum on his estate in Sarasota, was not by an Italian artist, but in reference to the giant paintings by Peter Paul Rubens, called by a misnomer,

Cartoons. In the estimation of this author, these were the most spectacular paintings I have ever beheld. The driving force behind this obsession was the fact John wanted to be known as, not just the circus man, but also a gentleman of refinement and taste. When visiting the art galleries and museums of New York, Venice, Berlin, Vienna, London, etc. He became a connoisseur of art, albeit, primarily self-taught. By no means a fool and realizing his limitations in the area of art appraisals, he became friends with—and eventually hired on a commission basis—a German gentleman by the name of Julius W. Bohler. He had spent most of his life buying and selling precious art objects and acting on behalf of other wealthy collectors.

Spending time in Europe buying and selling, but mostly buying, great works of art was Ringling's new fascination, and would eventually be the catalyst that brought about his falling on hard times. Of course, this was not the only thing. Other problems would happen, as it usually does when a great scion of the American scene comes undone.

As enumerated above, there were reasons John entertained this new passion. Being known as the circus man was something he did not entirely welcome, even though he did not overtly reject the title. His associations with influential personages in New York, and in the old world of Europe, gave him an ambition to be one of them. They were wealthy, and immersed in the prodigious trappings of all the things money could buy. It seemed to John the one thing they had and he had not, was *prestige*. In his mind, buying beautiful works of art that may have graced the castles, mansions, and other abodes of kings and noblemen of the past would bring him a spillover of esteem. Yet, trying to enter this realm of what he thought of as greatness and respect, would only be an ephemeral exercise in futility.

John had not come to the point of realization that most of these people had been born into far greater wealth then he. They were transported into their lifestyle because of their familial ties and their friends were of the same ilk. Moreover, the interests of their colleagues coincided with their own. What John had not and never would realize, was his time on this earth was worth far greater rewards than most all of the people he kept trying to cultivate, put together. Millions of people all over the United States and Europe, because of him, had experiences unequaled in the emotional rush attending a circus would give, or even the anticipation of the big top coming to town.

Ringling's Private Rail Car

Europe, Italy, Venice

The mode of travel to Europe was imbued in luxury and viewed with enthusiasm by Mable. The ocean-going liners of the day were the epitome of elegance and class. Primary ships were the R. M. S. Aquitania and the R. M. S. Mauritania. The passengers were pampered in an obscene way. John, in his inimitable manner, showed a great amount of impatience. Travel was just something to endure. Thus, the Ringling's, when traveling in the

United States, always went in style, going so far as to have in their possession a luxurious railroad car.

Venice, Italy

Mabel Ringling   **Saint John's Square**

The water taxi carried an exuberant John and Mable through the many canals and waterways in Venice until they reached the Grunewald Bauer Hotel. Here they would stay while both of them delighted and fulfilled their psyches with the rich history surrounding them.

Only steps away from Saint Marks Square, they rapidly made their way to The Piazza San Marco, initially to shop the various salons bordering the piazza, but what they found when they arrived were two orchestras playing waltzes by Johann Strauss in opposite sides of the square. Untold gorgeous architecture, many hundreds of years old, filled their eyes with complete wonderment and excitement. With a wild abandonment and extreme courtly gesture, not of his nature, John turned to the love of his life, bowing in the manner gentleman in the long ago past must have done.

"Mrs. John Ringling, may I have the pleasure of this Waltz?"

Mable, with stunned acceptance, returned his bow with a curtsy of her own, her heart overfilling with love of her husband replied, "Mr. Ringling you may have this dance and I will cherish this moment in this place, in my heart for the rest of my life."

The music was the *Blue Danube Waltz*. They whirled and whirled while the music reached crescendo after crescendo and they were lifted to other worlds. This moment would never again be duplicated in their entire lives. Mable, ever the uncontested beauty wherever she went, made a stunning image in a flowing white dress that emphasized her tiny waist and made her well-formed derriere a point of interest. Under a large hat, you could see the flash of her extravagant dark eyes, framed by wisps of dark brown hair.

John, for his part, was ever the symbol of unabashed insolence. Standing six-foot, one-inch tall, ramrod straight, he had an air of condescension with a girth tending toward expansiveness–quite imposing in stature, to be sure. The other travelers and citizens could only stare at the couple in complete, enraptured silence.

Together, they toured the various high-end shops and bought various items, most anything that caught their attention. Whether it was old, new, or in-between, it did not matter, as long as they were pleased with the item, or items, they fancied. On this particular trip, the heavy buying would take place in Vienna where John would meet Julius Bohler. With his confidence placed in that very knowledgeable art connoisseur, they would be picking pieces from the old masters. John now had a new mission in mind. He wanted to bring to Sarasota a grand art museum on the scale of anything that could be found anywhere in the country, yeah, even the world.

Vienna

Palais Dorotheum Auction House

Vienna, Austria

When they arrived in Vienna, they were met by Bohler, and together, they traveled to a trusted art auction where John and Mable intended to purchase rare paintings from prestigious estates that had fallen on hard times, which meant they had to raise capital to pay the ubiquitous taxes on their holdings.

The Palais Dorotheum Auction House is the oldest and most well organized and well-attended auction house in Europe and Ringling's arrival brought the major art director, J'on Eitter von Sörster, front and center. Mr. Sörster was aware Ringling would be a major buyer at this auction and made sure all courtesies were extended to him throughout this auction, targeting certain pieces in John's direction. Knowing what he was interested in was important to the success of this sale. Having a lifetime of dealing with the other side of life, prepared John for the frauds sure to occur wherever gigantic amounts of money were involved. This was no exception. The director approached Julius, John, and Mable, directing his oratory to Bohler, whom he knew to be the arbiter where paintings of noted artists would be exhibited for John. He pointed to the painting in the catalog and described to Bohler the characteristics of this masterpiece in extravagant terms. Bohler, caught up in the charisma and effectiveness of the director's oratory, seemed completely mesmerized by this piece of artwork and highly recommended it. They looked over at John, expecting some kind of response, but none came for some time, the silence rather enervating. Finally, he stood up, and with flushed face and angry flashing eyes, revealed another side of John Ringling.

"I am greatly disappointed in both of you. You, Mr. Sörster, for not revealing the full background of this painting and you, Mr. Bohler, for not attending to what I would consider a significant amount of homework. Let me point out to both of you gentlemen, there is cloud of uncertainty concerning this painting. Apparently, I was the only one who knew of the shortcomings of this piece of art. You see, gentlemen, about two years ago I attended an auction where this same art was presented for sale. It was never sold, because of a tainted background. It seems this painting may not have been painted by the Great Michelangelo, but may have been created by one of his talented students."

John decided to pass on that work of art. However, in the future he was able to purchase the very same piece at a giveaway price. Later, it was determined to be a genuine work by the master himself. We must remember, because of Ringling's experience, he was the quintessential risk taker, and this time it paid handsome dividends. Many times, John would go where no man had gone before and that experience proved once again, in most matters, it was best to rely on himself. Consequently, in the future, Bohler occupied a position of much less importance in Ringling's acquisition of art, and as the years passed and both men fell upon hard times, recriminations occurred, eventually causing a complete parting of the ways.

∞∂∞

John Ringling had many interests all over the United States. Whenever an investment presented itself and he thought he could make a buck, he bought it, to hell with properly registering the title, the hell with finding the right people to run the damn thing. He bought things such as short line railroads,

Winners and Losers

gold mines, oil wells, property in the wilderness, and interests in other businesses that might or might not turn a profit. The circus, however, was the one thing that was well run and earned an immense amount of capital and that circus was the basis of John's wealth.

As John expanded the circus, his brothers had a bad habit of expiring and suffering untimely deaths, putting the onus on John to run the entire operation, which he proved to be the equal of for a while.

Eventually, becoming enamored with the Florida location, Sarasota, he decided to try to make that city and area the equal of the upscale colonies on the east coast of Florida—Saint Augustine, Palm Beach, Fort Lauderdale, and Miami. With that in mind, Ringling acquired prodigious amounts of real estate. He proceeded to obtain land on the coast, but also bought real estate on nearby Islands, called Siesta Key and Longboat Key. (Key was a derivative of the Spanish word Cayo, or island reef.) The dream was to build luxurious hotels and sumptuous high-end homes for what he thought would be an invasion of his wealthy northern contacts, yet would never materialize. The mistake John made was believing they were his friends. Ever the promoter, John was not a fisherman, and couldn't care less about the high seas, but still acquired yachts he would use to give excursions to prospective buyers of his properties along the Sarasota coast.

Vidofiner II

Wethea

A chilling prognosticator of the eventual collapse of the Ringling dynasty could be divined by the horrific demise of the playthings he placed so highly and with so much pride in owning and displaying. Having one of the biggest yachts on the coast was a matter of intense pride to John. The first vessel acquired in 1913 was named *Wethea*, and eventually was replaced in 1917 by the 110-foot *Vidofiner II* that exploded and burned in 1920 while in for repairs and having its fuel tanks filled, seriously burning the chief engineer and killing one young crewmember.

After renting a prestigious yacht named the *Pastime* from the wealthy Wannamaker family of New York, he then pirated the look of the *Pastime* and built a new, 125-foot vessel called *Zalophus* with six staterooms and other areas for the crew and servants. This boat met its demise in 1930 off Lido Key when it hit an underwater rock and sank. It eventually was reported some ten years later, a total of ten passengers escaped, some with minor injuries, the only thing salvaged from the wreck, its engines. At the time of the accident, it was reported only 4 passengers and crew were aboard and all survived. The mystery occurred when survivors refused interviews and would not talk about this horrendous accident. That seemed a little strange. Ten years went by before the real story came out.

Al Smith

Betty Compton

Jimmy Walker

Winners and Losers

Jimmy Walker, the turbulent mayor of New York and friend of the Ringling's, was one of the survivors, but what was surprising is his traveling companion, a Ziegfeld Follies chorus girl, and actress named Betty Compton. Walker later divorced his wife to marry Betty in 1932.

In a corruption scandal, Jimmy Walker—who was a songwriter before becoming mayor of New York—wrote a popular song of the day, "Will you love me in December (as you did in May)?" was accused of accepting money from businessmen seeking favorable contracts from the city and he was forced, on September 1st, 1932, to resign, with pressure from President Franklin Roosevelt. Parties increased in the palatial Ca' d'Zan, at the time that John was pushing his multiple real estate ventures and the Yacht, *Zalophus*, now came into its own. The Ringling's not only used it to transport prospective buyers, but in other capacities as well. Important dignitaries utilized the vessel as their boudoir while enjoying John's hospitality. Other times when there was dancing under the extravagant moon and stars on the piazza by the bay, the orchestra would play from the deck of the Zalophus. This was John's personal Venice, his vision of San Marco Square.

As the participants arrived, they were conducted through aspirant gates that harked back to the European days of nobility and passed through on a winding road embellished with statuary imported from Europe. The automobiles were met by uniformed men, who would escort the arrivals into the receiving room, where they were greeted and presented with a memento of their visit to this palace. This would have to be considered one of the most lavish and innovative homes in America. John wanted to make each visit for his guests unforgettable in every way. He wanted to make the attendees participants in his dream. His aspiration was to make Sarasota the Palm Beach of the west coast of Florida, with *his* planned developments leading the way.

Butlers continued leading the guests into the grand living room, where finger-food was served and having them imbibe the refreshment of their choice. Even though this was the era of prohibition, Ca' d'Zan kept a healthy choice of banned beverages on hand.

John and Mable did not make their grand entrance until the guests were seated and were partaking in casual conversation. So as not to give the impression of royalty entering, they would join the festivities one at a time. Usually Mable was the first entrant, waving energetically to everyone who was there, but going immediately to the largest cultch of ladies. As was usually the case in that day and age, men and women clustered in each other's company to discuss the important issues of the day that were of interest to them.

∞∂∞

One person of overwhelming fascination to all of the ladies, and of course, all of the men present, was the actress Betty Compton. She accompanied the mayor of New York, Jimmy Walker, to this rendezvous. A member of Ziegfeld Follies, she appeared in the original stage production of *Funny Face* (1927) alongside Fred Astaire and Adele Astaire, as well as *Oh, Kay!* In 1926. Mable, being her usual ebullient self, hugged the actress.

"I am so glad you could make it to our little get together. I am sure the trip was very tiring, but you look so fabulous. Tell me how you do it. Generally, after a trip from New York I am not in any condition to meet people."

"The trip was not exhausting at all. It was an uplifting experience. Consider what the conditions were when I left the Great White North and then arrived in this land of palm trees and sunny beaches. How would it be possible to be tired and not excited after entering this enchanted home?"

"Believe me the enchantment is all mine, just meeting you and looking upon the person who was such a hit in the latest musical on Broadway. I'm absolutely thrilled."

Secretly, Mable was a little disapproving of being a party to the affair between Betty and Jimmy Walker, but John was the culprit in this episode. Mable did not linger long with Betty. She quickly included the other ladies in the room mostly in small talk. However, one subject near and dear to her heart, her most insidious and ever nascent, Old World rose garden would always be brought up in any conversation in which Mable was a participant. Much of her time was consumed in the care and feeding of her pride and joy.

After a proper interval, John made his appearance. You would have thought John would make sure a grand staircase was built, flowing into the giant living area, but, alas, there was one, but not of an imposing nature. He still made a rather compelling entrance transported from the upper floor in a rare accoutrement of the very wealthy, an elevator. His imposing size and straight carriage always made his entrance grand. His demeanor and manner of speaking, softly and infrequently, also commanded a measure of respect. On this evening, he made up his mind to be more solicitous toward his guests than was his wont.

∞∂∞

The Florida land boom had come to a paralyzing end in 1927. This event, and the 1929 stock market implosion, had a deleterious effect on the Ringling finances. Just before the market crash, he, in a juxtaposition of an improper business venture, bought the American Circus, lock stock and barrel.

Now, his position was that of a huckster. His income had been drastically reduced. The upscale hotel John was building, the Ritz Carleton, had to be abandoned, and was in an unfinished state. An explosion of beautiful statuary—art pieces purchased on the continent and meant for this grand hotel—populated the site as well as his estate. The museum had not as yet been opened.

An Aerial View of the Unfinished Ritz-Carlton Hotel at the Southern-end of Longboat Key

The Unfinished Ringling Ritz Carlton (1959)

More bad news was yet to come. John had no way of knowing the stabilizing factor in his life, and much of his success, would unexpectedly pass away. Mable was the one entity that, whether he knew it or not, would be linked to his financial accomplishments.

∞∂∞

John passed pleasantly among his guests, distributing cigars hand-rolled in Tampa, engaging in conversation primarily extolling the virtues of his properties. In the morning these guests were slated to board the personal ill-fated *Zalophus* and tour the islands, called keys, where his properties were located.

Al Smith, using a strong resonant voice, still as vibrant as when he was running for President of these United States, called to John.

"For God sakes, John, why in the *hell* did you have to build this magnificent mansion in a southern locality that cost me the Presidency?" He proclaimed. This was said in jest.

"Hell, yes, Al. I had to find a place far enough away from New York where even Tammany Hall couldn't find me." (Tammany Hall was the power broker that brought Al Smith and Franklin Roosevelt to prominence).

Winners and Losers

Catching the ear of Jacob Wallenberg, Chief Executive Officer of the Enskilda Bank of Stockholm, and of J.P. Morgan Jr., one of the most powerful men on Wall Street, John continued, "For God-sakes, I am devoid of adjectives to describe the joy I feel, having you gentlemen here this evening."

"What the hell is not to like," J. P. intoned. "This is a virtual paradise. John, I had no idea this place was as sumptuous as it is, certainly the equal of the most extravagant homes in America."

"If I may," Jacob piped up, "obviously you have brought the architecture and culture of the old world to Florida. You definitely deserve praise for this undertaking. I am caught up in the illustrious way you are serving the state of Florida."

That's not all I am serving. If you gentlemen will follow me to my personal speakeasy and partake of the many delights you will find there, I believe our conversation will become more animated.

Dining Room   **Per ballare sotto le stelle**   **Ca' d'Zan Tap Room**

The small tap room at Ca' d'Zan was a source of pride for John and it was certainly a place that gave off an air of unrespectability—with its muted lighting and multi-colored, mirrored glass behind a beautiful, polished teak bar. This enclave–placed strategically between the dining room and the kitchen— gave an aura and set the mood for matters of importance by distinguished gentlemen.

John moved behind the bar and became the bartender for the evening. In so doing, he placed himself in the spotlight, the ringmaster, so to speak. As he conversed with one and then the other, he allowed his unbounded enthusiasm for Florida and the island keys to show. His power of persuasion was now being tested.

"John, the downturn currently being experienced here in Florida has already occurred on the continent," Jacob said. "We are in the throes of a slump that has far-reaching effects. Not the least of it being the shrinking of capital for investment."

"Not to belabor the point," Al Smith went on to say, "but if I had been elected, I certainly would have declared a state of emergency for Florida and I believe I could have mitigated much of the damage that has taken place. Hoover lacks the capability, because of his belief in a flawed and jaundiced view of the role of government in bringing about renewed energy in the economy. This of course is my judgment, but I believe every man in this room shares my view." The one person who did not share this view was J. P. Morgan Jr. and he spoke up in a very subdued and reasonable tone. "Al, I appreciate your passion, but, many times, it is better to let the natural flow of events take place rather than have government interference that can have unintended consequences. We have seen this course of events take place in the past."

"Wait a minute J. P.," Al countered. "Was your view the same when your father organized the consortium that broke the malaise of the stock market in 1907? I know you were too young to appreciate what was going on then, but I dare say, you would heartily agree with the motivations of your father today.

"Yes, it was, and is, true. Remember, what he organized was private, and did not involve the Government."

Ringling did not want the conversation to continue in this vein so, in order to alleviate this line of dialogue, he intoned an appositive approbation. "Gentlemen what has happened has happened and all the ruminations we could go on about will do no good. Look around yourselves. We are inundated with sunshine and luxurious and resplendent foliage. Do you really believe, deep in your hearts, most of America would not want to live in this place? That is the reason there will be a new boom here. The people who have the foresight to invest now will have made a wise and intelligent decision."

Mable entered the room without knocking and said impatiently, "John, dinner is being served," and impishly asked, "Do you prefer it served while it is in a state of readiness or when it is too cold to eat?"

"Gentlemen, follow your noses and I am sure you will find the dining room," John, properly chastised, proclaimed to "the boys."

An elegant meal ensued, served by a bevy of white-gloved waiters. The conversation was lively, and off in the distance, a band struck up on the deck of the *Zalophus*, preparing for the evening festivities. In the winter season, John would use the circus band to entertain his guests, and on this night, there would be dancing under a velvety sky, the guests inundated by the light of a silvery moon on the piazza by the bay.

All of this was done to prepare his guests for the journey they would take in the morning on his yacht the Zalophus, to observe, view, and listen to a sales pitch extolling the many virtues and attributes of the Ringling properties. During this trip, he would try to avert their eyes away from the unfinished and abandoned Ritz Carleton Hotel, certainly an anomaly of the first category. This was an element that showed the beginning cracks in the Ringling dynasty.

The bankers, J. P. Morgan and Jacob Wallenberg had been invited, not only to interest them in real estate, but to curry favor for loans needed in the future. At this time, little did John know how great his need for capital would become?

∞∂∞

Nineteen twenty-nine became a watershed year, notable for its negativity. The greatest love of his life passed away at a very young age, struck down because of Diabetes and Addison's disease. John was very morose and suicidal. Left with nothing, he was unable to turn to a close friend, because of his unbending, terse way of handling people and had not cultivated even one person in his entire life to act as a surrogate for Mable.

Following this catastrophe, the second resounding, unforeseen circumstance occurred. On October 28 and 29, 1929, the stock market crashed, signaling the end of the Roaring Twenties and the final nail driven into the coffin containing the remnants of the Gilded Age. These two days would forever be known as Black Monday and Black Tuesday.

We must remember, all of this became relevant after John had expended about one and a half million, most of it borrowed, buying the American Circus. This curious state of affairs came about after his loss of controlling interest in Madison Square Garden subsequently excluding him from the board of directors. The new board decided to award the dates John had for *his* circus to the aforementioned American Circus. John, for his part, made a tragic mistake. He bought the American Circus in order to claim the dates they had been awarded. This was not the first time his common sense was called into question.

Any of his mistakes in the past were covered up by the enormous amount of capital the circus represented. This was about to change, since the great depression was imminent. The profitably of the circus now declining, it still was profitable, but could no longer cover the huge amount of money John owed.

Life had to go on. Traveling for the circus, an onerous chore was a requirement. People who worked for him were aware of John becoming more and more distant. They noticed his eyes were mostly bloodshot and red rimmed. He spent an immense amount of time alone in his private railroad car. All of them worried he might take his own life. This never happened, but we will never know how close to the final solution he came.

John had become bicameral, in other words two personalities in one. One person was an outgoing, self-indulgent, fun-seeking adventurer, the other an imploding inwardly, sordidly morose, recluse. Searching for some kind of relief, he decided on a trip to Europe, hoping to escape the deep doldrums he was experiencing.

While in Amsterdam, he attended a celebratory, Fourth of July party being held for the edification of Americans living or traveling there. An annual festival, put forth by the King and Queen of the Netherlands would prove to be another disaster for the King of the Circus.

The orchestra was a curious mix of American and old-world European resonances that stuttered back and forth between Jazz and Waltzes trying to satisfy the whims of the attendees. Every time a Waltz played, memories of Mable came flooding back. John desperately wanted to dance and as he looked around, a particularly attractive blonde-haired beauty held his attention. With bated breath, he decided to approach her and request the honor of her presence on the dance floor. John of course had never been in the habit or the position of asking a stranger to dance with him. This was new, causing his pulse to raise a few beats. Approaching her he graciously asked, "Excuse this intrusion, but would you consent to be my partner for this dance?" She seemed to be in no particular hurry to accept his invitation and allowed a small interval of time to elapse before she made the commitment graciously to accede to his request. Moving about the dance floor with a lightness John did not expect, made him realize she was not a stranger to the world of dance. He, on the other hand, had an awkwardness that belied the fact that dancing and John were on speaking terms. Of course, in order to distract this participant of his from any ineptness on his part, he nervously started a conversation.

"Madam let me introduce myself. I am John Ringling. May I inquire as to what your name is?"

"Of course, my name is Emily Haag Buck. You know, Mr. Ringling, an introduction to you was not necessary. I make it a point to know who the attendees are and what they do. It's part of my nature I guess."

"In that area, please excuse my ignorance. I am apparently lacking many social skills. Well, if you know about me, I believe you should inform me about yourself."

"I will be more than happy to do so. You already know my name, so let us go from there. My home is New York City. I am divorced, and I am happily single. I do not have children, nor do I plan to have any in the future. As far as I am concerned, my education is complete. I graduated from a private, girl's school in upper New York state, and hope to God I never see one like it again."

"Tell me," John inquired. "You seem to have an unusual dislike for this school."

"It is not just that school, but *any* school which has unusual disciplinary codes of conduct. My mission in life is to have as much fun as it is possible to experience. That period of my life was very dark and foreboding. Let us not dwell on things that are long past, the future is beckoning and it is where I belong."

There was something about this girl that excited and held a fascination for John. His time in Europe was running short, so, after spending a few days gaily seeing the sights of Amsterdam and visiting more than one raucous nightclub with Emily leading the way, John embarked for home.

At least for a moment in time, Emily was able to bring a different dimension to his life. As soon as it was feasible, John again made contact with this wild thing who encompassed all the things Mable was not. Mable was down to earth and much grounded in her home and relatives. Emily did not care about home and relatives. The only people who counted in her life were the ones that were out and about, having fun and not giving a fig about tomorrow. Even the gorgeous home in Sarasota, Ca' d'Zan, meant nothing to her. She would rather be attending the parties with her erstwhile friends in New York and Palm Beach.

Winners and Losers

John Ringling eventually did the unthinkable and married Emily Haag Buck, a union that would become the final stone around his neck, hastening the crumbling of his empire.

John and Emily

The winds of change were gathering with hurricane force. John's income was diminishing and his creditors were howling for a piece of his failing dynasty. He tried desperately to extricate himself from the quagmire that was the result of his own folly. Correcting one of his mistakes, he divorced Emily after a court battle she bitterly contested. She tried to claim as many assets of John's estate as possible. This occurred during and after the divorce, and of course, claiming dower rights after his death, she did succeed in establishing control of valuable paintings stored in New York.

The Ringling's were divorced in July 1936 and John died in December 1936.

Married 1930, divorced 1936

Ringling suffered his first heart attack in the spring of 1932. Though the first, it would prove to be the final knell in the Ringling saga. One by one, his friends deserted him. Sometimes, the friends were discarded by John and other times the old friends jumped ship to save themselves, or, perhaps, it was their zeal to feed upon the remains of a once great empire.

As John descended into the hell of invalidism, he was no longer able to defend himself against the many wolves circling and closing for the kill. The circus attorney who John thought would give him good advice was now working with the opposition. Surprisingly the only one giving good advice was his ex-wife, Emily, who kept advising John to get another attorney, probably in an attempt to save as much of his assets as possible which would be in her own best interests.

The board of the circus with the acquiescence of his sister and sister's in-law deserted and deposed him of his position as Chief Operating Officer. They then elected Sam Gumpertz, a former friend of John's, and made him CEO of the operation of the circus. Imagine, if you can, these relatives, who had acquired their positions in the Ringling Brothers Circus because of the death of John's brothers—and had nothing to do with the day-to-day operations of the business—throwing out the guiding light, namely one John Nicholas Ringling, from the office of president of the Ringling Circus. Some of the vituperation directed John's way he had earned because of his obstreperous ways riding roughshod over the interested parties in the circus in the past, and doing what he wanted without consulting them.

The great success of this enterprise was achieved with humongous sacrifices by all of the brothers. The sisters-in-law rode the coattails and enjoyed the prosperity and luxurious living conditions the circus had provided. At this point, their attitude was ambivalence to an incapacitated brother. They were intent on protecting the remaining assets of the business."

Winners and Losers

John accommodated them. John died in December 1936. At his death, his total cash in the bank stood at three hundred and eleven dollars.

∞∂∞

Nevertheless, John Ringling's Estate was deemed to be worth twenty million dollars at the time of his demise. Ca' d'Zan and the Ringling Museum remained in limbo for ten years after his death, as a result of actions being fought out in the courts.

The terms of his will resulted in the state of Florida becoming the beneficiary and finally took possession in 1946, claiming back taxes were due and came before all other claims. This was after the property came to a state of shabbiness, making it almost unrepairable. The movie *Great Expectations* was filmed there because of the estate's poor condition. The museum and priceless works of art as of this writing, 2014, are rumored to be worth one billion dollars

John did have one sister, Ida Ringling North, with whom he had a falling out. She ended up, however, being a sweet and sour adversary and felt a love for him to the bitter end. Her son, John Ringling North, eventually bought and became the owner of The Greatest Show on Earth.

The Secret Garden

And, now, the final, unpleasant irony; John and Mable were never buried but kept in above ground unmarked vaults in New Jersey for over a half century. Finally, a court ordered their bodies, along with Ida Ringling North, be interred on the grounds of the Ringling home and museum in 1991. They narrowly missed being buried in a potter's field because the payment of fifty dollars per month was in arrears.

The Empty Crypts are Below the Statue of David to his Right and Left in the Museum

The Mystery as told to the author: John's sister's estate, Ida North, apparently had something to do with the bodies of John and Mable never being buried in the crypts in the museum. Her estate was insistent that Ida be buried with John and court action was taken to see that her desires were carried out. This turned out to be the final indignity and disrespect to a life lived as a winner, benefactor to a city and state, and philanthropist to an entire country.

Because of John Ringling and the State of Florida, you and I can enjoy his magnificent home, museum, and priceless works of art

For some reason, the bodies were buried in the dark of night, apparently to escape scrutiny by officials of the state, county, or city. It was possible that the proper licensing of the estate as a burial site had not been obtained or other reasons never enunciated. Docents working on the grounds of the Ringling Estate were instructed to not speak of the empty crypts, or the graves, or the location of the graves. They are simply noted on the map of the Ringling grounds as the "Secret Garden."

The crypts in the museum John had built specially for Mable and himself are still empty.

And Now ...

Adele Von Ohl Parker
Equestrian, Actress, Teacher
Star of the Buffalo Bill Wild West Show

To say I had much contact with Adele in her later years is like saying I had in my possession the Hope Diamond for a moment in time. It would be hard to think of anyone who lived a more exciting existence. She came into this life as Adele Von Ohl about 1883, in Plainfield, New Jersey, from parents that emigrated from Germany. At one time, they had quite a nice fortune, but they may have fallen on hard times. No one actually knows, but Adele was a well brought up young woman, as you would have assumed from her grasp of manners and her educated ways. If she had a failing, if one could call it that, it was her thirst for adventure and boldness when it came to risk taking.

Winners and Losers

Those of you that have unusually precocious and thrill seeking children, certainly know the trials and tribulations you endured while they were attaining the age of majority. In Adele's case, her parents must have had the endurance of missionaries and they guided her with a great deal of love. We know this from the love and respect Adele had for her parents all through her life.

Her parents owned a stable with truly blooded steeds and were instrumental in teaching Adele the fine art of horsemanship. Far be it for me to characterize a nationality, but Germans have always been known to exhibit traits of industriousness among others and Adele was certainly of the same character. By the time she had attained puberty, she was an unusually striking woman. At five-foot-six, she was taller than the average woman of that period. She was slender, but not thin, and no matter what she was attending to, cut an exceptionally attractive figure. Of course, she had deep chestnut hair with reddish highlights, very much like some of her favorite horses. Her face was oval, with all of her features uncommonly synchronized. The deep brown eyes that seemed to become liquid and darker when her mood was ratcheting down set off her well-formed nose. Oh yes, she also had a decidedly intimidating and almost violent temper if she found someone mistreating one of her equine charges. No one wanted to face one of her tongue-lashings. Even though she was mannerly most times, she could be as profane as a cowboy on the range when the need arose.

At an unusually tender age, she started doing chores for other people and learning how to make her own way in life. Many of her neighbors remembered, in later years, the fearless girl that took on chores that the boys would not consider. However, for all of the many things she had an interest in, it was always the horses, *ALWAYS THE HORSES*. She wanted to be with them twenty-four hours a day. When she was only a small tyke, she was on board spirited mounts that well versed riders would not dare ride. The horses seemed to have an affinity for Adele and she for them. Even in later years, spirituality existed between her and her mounts.

Because of her ebullient nature, and her command of language, probably her ability to speak German and English fluently, led her to speak a little of other languages. In that time, there was an enormous influx of immigrants, and it served her well. Naturally outgoing, she was exceedingly popular in school and that did not stop with one gender. It seems that the boys were particularly enthusiastic when they were in her presence, and extremely intimidated by her ability as a budding equestrian. The tricks she was able to do with a horse and the way she could get her charges to do her bidding, along with her natural beauty and popularity, made the boys have an extreme case of shyness. Yet, Adele would have none of the flirtatious moments that most young adults had at that age. Her entire being, focused on the great equestrian she was becoming and her love for the stage.

As she was growing up, she was actively sought after to participate in school and local stage venues. We must remember, at the turn of the 20th century, entertainment consisted of stage, vaudeville, minstrel shows, fairs, circuses, picnics, and the simple gathering of friends at each other's homes. Motion pictures had recently been invented, so that was not a viable option at that time. As you can see, it was a much simpler, and to my way of thinking, a beautiful time, *if* you were one of the lucky ones who owned a home and a piece of land where you could have the ability to be self-sufficient. Adele had all of these things, but, more relevant to her, she was able to do the one thing she loved above all others, to ride her beloved horses. She also valued her ability to teach others to appreciate the art of horsemanship as well.

It seems, when we have achieved a certain level of success in a particular field, we then feel free to give advice to other people in that field of endeavor, even if it is unwanted. Of course, in Adele's case, she was well qualified to provide leadership and advice to up and coming novices and it would serve her well in later years when her real joy was teaching children the fine art, not only of horsemanship, but of life itself. If there was anyone more qualified to expound upon life and its various ramifications then I would not know who. As this story is presently written, you will certainly come to the same conclusion as I, that this one, wild, and in many ways, exemplary life, is one worth knowing.

Adele, when not working at the ranch, which was time consuming and for a normal teen exhausting, started acting in plays that were produced in her area. Suddenly, she found her second love, that of being a thespian. The *Plainfield Courier News* carried an article by their theatrical critic that was highly complementary. The critic wrote, "Adele Von Ohl's first appearance as a professional actress might be considered a triumph, she carried herself as a professional."

I suppose her naturally outgoing ways, and wanting to inject her personality into everything around her, led to the gift she had for self-promotion. That character trait finally led to the stage and ultimately to New York, where she became one the highest paid actors before the bright lights of Broadway. That was so long ago, Adele hardly talked about that period of her life. So many of the details have been lost, but I'm sure somewhere along the way, it occurred to her, why not combine the two loves, and start exhibiting the wonderful, exciting, and dangerous tricks on a horse she had perfected when she was scaring the daylights out of friends and acquaintances at her parent's home. This led to an audition with none other than the Barnum Circus at Madison Square Garden. It was not long before her performance was center ring and where she acquired the addiction to tumultuous crowds and adoring fans. She performed sometime later with the Ringling Circus, of course center ring.

On a first name basis with many of the Ringling brothers, especially Albert Ringling—the only one of the Ringling brothers who was a true performer, along with his wife, Louise, also a skilled equestrian—a wonderful relationship developed. It was Al who brought Big Bill Cody, a.k.a. Buffalo Bill, to the circus to view a fabulous new entertainer who was an incredible rider and magical thespian.

Attention was drawn her way, not just because of her talent and beauty, but also because of the many other attributes she exhibited. We must remember, if you were in the circus, you had no latitude to defer the many chores that all performers had to attend to. Adele would take the dirtiest jobs in stride. Because of this lack of ego and her naturally effusive nature, other workers wanted to become her friend. She had one other characteristic that was exceedingly welcome among the workers, performers, and management; she was accepting and not critical of the flaws of other people, whether she was having interaction with the Bearded Lady or Tiny Tim, the smallest person in the world.

Many of the participants in the circus were gathered from Europe, especially the acrobats and high wire acts. Adele's fluency in German, because of her background and heritage, held her in excellent stead with the heavily accented leanings of the European circus troupes.

Winners and Losers

About this time, I believe, she became friends with a little spit of a girl from Ohio called Annie Oakley, who was already famous as an expert marksman and trick shooter. She usually performed with her one love, her husband, and was now forming a new show and planning to leave the Wild West troupe, albeit with the muted blessing of Big Bill Cody. The two would remain friends for life. Annie decided to approach Cody and relate to him the accomplishments of this wild and superb horsewoman, now appearing with the Ringling Circus. However, Cody was far ahead in this matter and had personally observed Adele's wild and bizarre act; this was because of Al Ringling's invitation to view her performance. Big Bill sent his personal agent to offer her a contract.

Nobody knows what the terms were, but they were generously sufficient and Adele gave notice to Al Ringling of her impending departure from his circus and he was gracious enough to send her off with the warmest regards and best wishes. Now, she began a fantasy life of travel to Europe, England, France, and various places that Adele had only dreamt about. They were met with thunderous applause and an adulation that was reserved for royalty, and yes, they had performed for the King and Queen of England and other well-known European personages.

After their return, or possibly while still in France, the show was joined by a new personality that had many and various skills, one of his chief attributes being his complete disregard for his own personal safety. The brashness he displayed in the show was contrary to his seemingly benign personality when not performing. Nobody seemed to know anything about him, and because of his penchant of keeping to himself and holding his own council, he was hard to get to know. Evidently, Bill Cody knew him before he joined the show. It would behoove you to know that Big Bill was acquainted with most of the noted western cowboys of his time and became friends with many of them, whether or not they had been involved in nefarious activities.

Jim Parker was the name of this person as presented at the time. I personally believe he was a. k. a. Robert Leroy Parker, better known as the infamous outlaw, *Butch Cassidy*. Butch had been made famous by the latest movie that claimed Butch and the Sundance Kid had died in a shootout in Bolivia, but there was no evidence that came forward to prove that scenario, including DNA on the bodies where they supposedly were buried. However, several people came forward and claimed they were in contact with Butch in later years, including his sister and a book authored by a person who claimed he *was* Butch Cassidy.

Winners and Losers

Robert Leroy Parker aka Butch Cassidy and Adele

The author of that book made the claim he had returned to France and had surgery to change his appearance. If all this is true, what better place to go incognito than the Buffalo Bill Wild West Show, where he could earn an excellent living doing the things he did best with his intimate knowledge of the Wild West and his abilities of horsemanship, roping, and shooting, while shielded by his good friend, Big Bill? I realize that the forgoing is a mighty big stretch, but, as you will see, going forward, with the story of Adele Von Ohl Parker, this whole picture will become much clearer.

One small aside. Who was the unknown mystery woman named Etta Place who traveled with Butch and Sundance to South America and then back to New York at about the same time that the Wild West Show returned to America? This just adds to the mystery and I will leave it to the reader to use his or her imagination.

It would only be in the realm of reality that Adele had a few loves along the way, but we will never know. Adele never talked about her past loves in my presence, except to make a few deprecating remarks about her husband. She was drawn to "Jim Parker." His quiet ways created an aura of mystery about him and they had many things in common, primarily his ability to throw caution to the wind and perform exciting feats of daring on a mount. A certain amount of rivalry must have existed between them, of course, but this only added to the allure of the relationship. However, the one thing that attracted Adele was the one factor among others that eventually would force them apart … his extreme masculinity!

Parker's life had been filled with adventurous flings and a thirst for the expensive and raucous times that he had experienced in an earlier era. It was an addiction he would never overcome. As time went on, however, the constant travel and living out of a suitcase began to wear on both of them, especially Adele, and she began to relish the idea of settling down. A thought of marriage, along with its possibility of a stable home and being in one place, was beginning to appeal to her. Her parents, who absolutely detested Jim, proved the greatest problem. Parents have a knack for insight that their children do not always possess. Together with her parents advancing age and the income that Adele provided on a periodic basis, made them fear, not only Adele's future, but also their own.

Jim Parker had a strong desire to go west, the West that he knew well coupled with a hankering to *go home*. He knew that they were doing cowboy movies in California from contacts with many of his friends who were now acting in western movies, friends like, William S. Hart, Bat Masterson, and Wyatt Earp, among others.

Jim and Adele married about 1909, in Detroit, Michigan. Soon after, they began making plans to depart the Wild West Show and strike out for the far West. They had money and Bill Cody's show was declining in popularity, abetted by his inclination for nipping from the bottle. Investments he had at that time were not going well and he certainly was not giving the attention the show needed at a time when other forms of entertainment were intruding and taking attendees away.

Now the odyssey begins, with great expectations and much trepidation: First, they had to arrange their mode of transportation, their first consideration the horses, highly trained performing horses and their backups. Then came the usual household items, which were many, considering the way they had to live while with the show, not to mention their extensive wardrobe. Last, but not least, they had to say farewell to the delightful friends they had made, accompanied with many tears and much heartbreak. These were not just acquaintances, but people that they had close personal relations with on an unusually intimate basis. These were people they traveled with, many times sleeping in tents, dining together, sharing with them their innermost thoughts, having laughs in good times, shedding tears and commiserating with them when life handed them it's cruelest vengeful performances. When times were at their worst, they could always rely on one another. Fortunately, money was not a problem, so their mode of transportation was not a major consideration I believe they chose the train as the best way to go, considering the many various and sundry things they had to bring along.

The trip was long and exhausting and not something to be excited about, considering the travel and the things they had been through in the last few years. Nevertheless, they were filled with anticipation, looking forward to what the future held. Because of their many contacts in show business, they had no worries in finding a position at their destination. Producers and directors had been in contact with them over the last few months. The silent movies were exploding and the need for all types of personnel was essential. However, the need for stuntmen in the Western's was acute, leaving Jim and Adele in the enviable position of being able to name their own terms, yet never realizing the full impact of what they would have to endure.

The producers and directors of silent movies were in a hurry to "get the celluloid in the can," so to speak, to satisfy the public's thirst for their fare. Cost was also a consideration, so that meant working many long hours. Considering the type of work they did, exhaustion was a factor, as well as the many injuries they suffered. Adele continued to perform the many stunts that were required with hands or arms that were broken, not to mention concussions, infections, headaches and various other ailments, but, as it were, *the show must go on.*

About this time, her marriage started on a downward tilt. Jim, reverting to the wild ways of yore, found the temptations of the movies, with the many beautiful and rather promiscuous, devilish women he encountered, too much for his salaciousness and weak moral compass.

Suddenly, Jim decided to visit friends in Montana. As it turned out, they were involved in rounding up presumably wild horses. It required building fences, as well as taking care of and breaking barely manageable stallions and mares. Needing help desperately, Jim turned to the one person who could solve this problem, *Adele*. However, she had no inclination to be with Jim again. He, with much fervor, begged for her help. Considering what she was going through as a "stuntman" (she performed stunts for the male Western stars of the day; hence the male use of the term), she started to consider his proposal and finally ended up with Jim in the wild hinterlands of Montana.

Thomas Edwin   **William S. Hart**   **(Tom Mix)**

Of course, this was a huge mistake. She found that the hours were long and breaking wild horses was not exactly what her idea of a career should be.

Eventually, with Jim's dearth of business acumen, Adele found the money running out. She then turned to the thing that gave her pleasure ... working with horses. Adele started organizing her own Wild West Show, with herself as the featured performer. She actually went to the reservations to recruit Indians, as well as to ranches looking for equipment, buckboards, and old stagecoaches. She additionally enticed other ex-show people to join her small coterie of performers. She was, of course, a dreamer, for the days of the Western Wild West Shows were truly dead.

The show made a few stops in small towns along the way with highly disappointing results. She arrived in Cleveland, with hopes of making enough money to get the show to the next stop. It was there they were scheduled to appear at the Palace Theater. This would have been a high-profile engagement and may have led to better bookings in the future *if* they would have received encouraging newspaper revues. For one reason or another, the

Palace canceled the show. Adele now found herself in a predicament that put the responsibility on her to find places for the performers to stay. What do you do with a band of Indians that were still a little wild, and animals that had to be taken care of? To make matters worse, Adele did not have enough money for her next meal. Fortunately, through her many years on the road, she had made many friends. She dispersed what was left of the ensemble still with her, to various ranches in the Cleveland area that generously made their facilities available. With her indomitable will coming to the forefront, she decided that her next calling would be teaching children the art of horsemanship.

Through one ruse or another, she managed to get reporters from the various newspapers in Cleveland to interview her and announce the start of her riding academy. The reporters were more than happy to do so, given Adele's storied background. She went on to establish the most well-known and unusual ranch in Ohio, called Parkers Ranch, but to the people that truly mattered, it was referred to it as Paradise. Her ranch was situated on the edge of the vast Cleveland Metropolitan park system, called Cleveland's "Emerald Necklace." Over the next forty years, Adele taught thousands of lucky children to become equestrians as well as ladies and gentlemen.

Never again would she live with Jim Parker, but, for some reason, she kept his last name. As far as I know, he returned to Parkers Ranch only one time, this time acting much as the careless, wild Butch Cassidy would have behaved. Much to Adele's consternation, he was drunk and flashing guns, threatening to shoot everybody within shouting distance. It finally took the police chief of North Olmstead, Ohio, assisted by a few deputies, to remove him from the premises. Adele never heard from him again. Nevertheless, the fear he would return was a constant torment she endured.

Winners and Losers

She went on to hold Wild West Shows on her ranch every year, and the performers were all the children, or former students, that had become fine, upstanding adults. Over the years, all of them proclaimed that much of their success in life was due to the training they had received from Adele. Everyone associated with the ranch eagerly awaited that event, some in anticipation and others with some trepidation and consternation, because of the youth of the performers. However, each time they pulled off the show with aplomb, or should I say with shaky assurance.

It is not my intention to relate the many vagaries of the ranch. There are books written on this subject, enumerating all of the idiosyncrasies of that institution. A book of which I *will* make mention is entitled, *The Search for Adele Parker*, a book I recommend highly. My purpose in writing this is to give life to Adele's early days, which, in my estimation, must have been exciting and fabulous. I have inserted some mystery in her life when I interjected Butch Cassidy as possibly her husband. Is my rendition true? I do not believe anyone can disprove it beyond a doubt nor, for that matter, prove what I have felt was a real and possible scenario. The many things of which I have written are what I felt actually happened, but the passage of time has precluded that result as actual fact.

I personally knew Adele when I was a young man. We had many conversations, and in my rush to grab life, I did not listen as I should have. Now, I lament the hedonistic ways of youth.

Ron Chicone

Certainly, a woman as iconoclastic as Adele was a person worthy of all the accolades thrown her way. Let me reiterate that she *was a personage and a dignitary* well worth knowing.

As Adele Von Ohl Parker neared death in 1969, she approached it as she had other great moments in her life—with anticipation and eagerness. Her thought would have been, "Let's get it on and go forward to the next great journey," She knew it to be a grand adventure.

And the show goes on!

Jekyll Island Club
The Millionaire's Enclave
Exclusivity was Its Province

F or every season a time, for every time an age, for every age a reason. Beauty is not a constant for every individual. I can only speak for myself when I speak glowingly about this island on the Georgia coast.

Please allow me to rescind that statement. This beautiful place will live in the eyes, the mind, the heart of *anyone* who has ever seen a majestic oak, over- flowing with Spanish moss, eyes that can behold the immense vista of marshland, teeming with the treasures of the sea, vast areas that bring the palms and the various Old South flora into spectacular view, and a mind that goes to a level of complete relaxation because of surroundings that are surreal. You have just entered the lowlands of the Deep South.

In this chapter, I am asking you to stay and visit for a while, and allow the ghosts that are so plentiful to invade your reverie. As you let your mind open, you will meet the extremely wealthy, the idle rich, and others who were the industrialists that made our nation into the savior of the free world.

Union Club 1860

Union Club Ball Room

The old New York Union Club is the second oldest gentleman's club in America, established in 1836 and the impetus of the evolution of The Jekyll Island Club. The New York Club was, by any definition, truly palatial.

Outside stairs controlled the entrance that was patrolled by security guards that generally did not require your identification; your personage was instantly recognized and you were shown into the sitting room, where the members would hold sway with whatever the political ramifications of the day was occurring. This room was generally called the B. S. room and much of it was tossed around in this venue:

Members of some note were:

- John Jacob Astor IV – Titanic victim
- Dwight D. Eisenhower – President of the United States
- Ulysses S. Grant – Civil War General and President of the United States
- William Randolph Hearst – Newspapers and owner of Hearst Castle
- Leonard Jerome – Grandfather of Winston Churchill
- J. P. Morgan – Financier
- Winfield Scott – General of the Army
- Philip Sheridan – General of the Army
- William T. Sherman – General of the Army
- Cornelius Vanderbilt – Shipping and Railroads

Many others of rather impressive pedigree attended this club. One of the noteworthy articles of faith included the fact that members who belonged to the Confederacy were never expelled or forced to give up their memberships. Consequently, these Southern members were all too familiar with the Georgia coast, and almost certainly were the go-to-guys when discussing investments regarding land to purchase when establishing hunting and fishing reserve in the South.

One of the members never included in talks about establishing a southern reserve was William Tecumseh Sherman. Even 20 years after the end of the "War Between the

States," animosity still ran high among not only southern sympathizers, but also some northern members, who almost certainly had relatives living in the Confederacy and could not easily forget the scorched earth destruction visited on the South by Sherman. He was easily the most reviled survivor of that war. He did not mind being excluded, because he had no intention of returning to an area where his life could have been in danger.

The members of the Union Club had given thought to having a retreat for hunting and fishing almost from the time the New York Club was formed. After the war, the way became clearer because of reconstruction in the south. Pardon the pun, but, at this time, land was dirt-cheap. Money was not of importance, however, in the Union Club's acquiring land for the development of hunting and fishing grounds, the right piece of property was of the utmost importance. They had been casting about in all directions and not coming up with anything that caught their fancy.

One evening, as they sat in the BS room, or in the nicer parlance of the day, "The Lounge," John Pierpont Morgan was holding court as he often did, Members gave him much leeway because of his extraordinary success in matters of finance, and much influence, not only in the hierarchy of the administration in Washington, but around the world. He was a rather large and rotund man with a red, bulbous nose that was large and prominent because of rosacea. This did not detract from his commanding presence. On this evening, cigar smoke was thick in the atmosphere of the room; Morgan was conversing with a gentleman who sported a rather bushy beard, a cigar, and a jigger of bourbon on the table next to him.

"Ulysses, are you going to get on board with our project of a southern encampment?" he asked.

The eighteenth President of the United States flicked the ash of his cigar into an ashtray and responded, "I'm all for the membership of this club acquiring this thing that you have been pumping for years, but, you know Morgan, I'm getting along in years, and I do prize my comfort. In my lifetime, I've had enough roughing it, to last me until I die. So you boys have a nice time with this little project, but count me out. However, if I can be of help, you can depend on me."

A committee had been formed some time ago to pursue this project, and as yet, had not met with any success. William Cutting, a real estate magnate who was listening interjected.

Newton Finney   **Ulysses Grant**   **J. P. Morgan**

"I know of a member who may be of some help, by the name of Newton Finney, He has some business interests in coastal Georgia. I believe he is in the billiards room playing Bottle Pool."

That particular game was one of the favorites of the Union Club. The club had recently changed its bylaws and allowed women to step in to positions that were formerly held by men and the post of concierge was now held by a lovely and ingratiating woman. She immediately summoned Mr. Finney and he languidly strolled into the lounge. When asked about land that might be obtained in the south, it instantly piqued his interest.

As fate would have it, his brother in-law had recently inherited an Island on the Georgia coast called Jekyl Island that his family had owned for about 100 years. This timely bit of news was instantly relayed to the other members in the lounge. J. P. asked the location, and was vaguely informed that it was south of Savannah. J.P. then turned to Sheridan and asked him, if he knew of anyone who was familiar with the Savannah Area.

"I certainly do," Sheridan said. "I will talk to William Hardee. He was the Confederate General who opposed Sherman's march to the sea." With that, members waited to receive further information from Finney. In the meantime, Sheridan communicated with Hardee's children (Hardee by this time had passed away) and they informed him "Jekyl Island was a prized piece of real estate that had everything the members were looking for. Finney later informed them the Island could be obtained for the rather steep price of $125,000.

A few members had private yachts, and this gave them an excuse to mount a mission to Jekyl Island, as it was then spelled, later changed to Jekyll. This mission was partly funded by the Union Club and the balance by the members themselves and it ended up being quite an armada of people, but well worth the trip.

When the armada returned and informed the members what they had encountered, their enthusiasm knew no bounds, and they immediately set about creating the documents of purpose and incorporation, with an initial 53 members that would grow to the maximum number of 100.

Purpose

To own and maintain a hunting, fishing, yachting, and general sporting resort, to promote social intercourse among its members and their families, and to carry out such other purpose, authorized by its charter, as may be determined by the Board of Directors, Jekyl Island Club Officers, members, Constitution, Bylaws, and Charter book. So read the words of the official charter.

Winners and Losers

An architect and construction company was hired forthwith, and construction was started in 1886, and completed in 1888. The building was an immense and beautiful structure, designed by Charles Alexander of Chicago that complemented the tastes of the Victorian era. Many problems were encountered in building this edifice, such as finding and hiring of laborers. Skilled craftsmen had to be imported from the North and building supplies transported by ship. Its remote location necessitated building roads to the site, so the importation of horses, mules, carts and wagons had to be undertaken, along with the implements and mechanics to keep it all running smoothly. Tents and temporary housing, medical facilities, chefs, cooks and tons of food had to be imported, gardens established, and eventually, this magnificent structure arose from the heavily forested island.

By the 1930's, the members considered this building hopelessly outdated, and if the money had been available would have torn it down and replaced it with what would have been considered a more modern edifice. Funny, what goes around comes around. It's now revered and considered priceless.

Buildings come and go, but this building captures the imagination, the spirit, the eternal quest that exists in all of us for a time in the past we can no longer visit, and wish we could go back in time and live in this creation just one moment in that bygone age, a time when you dressed for dinner, men wore ties to play golf, woman wore hats with a flair that no longer exists, inter- personal relationships were paramount, picnics were done with panache, "elegance surrounded everything they did". In every one of us that glimmer of sophistication is still there.

Members matriculated to this enclave, generally, for about three or four months. The weather was exquisite in the winter months—January, February, and March were the preferred season—but many members came down in November. To northerners coming out of the cold and snow, this had to seem like heaven. Add to this the lure of hunting and fishing, tennis, golf, bicycling and many other appealing pursuits.

One other activity was carried on in the dining room, card room, poolroom, or out on the beautiful veranda; "the pursuit of money," adding to the members' many millions. This endeavor was one never talked about openly, that would have been considered the height of indiscretion. Many of the largest deals this country has ever seen were consummated at this club, including a highly secret meeting that created the Federal Reserve, the ramifications of which were, and are, felt worldwide.

The Club as it looked in the late 1800's

Today

The Member Cottages

Members of this club lived an existence that can only be described as high-wide, and handsome, and of course, the club itself was not enough to satisfy their desire for living in a way the very wealthy felt would be the *least* of what they would expect if they were home. That meant servants, but they never used that word, preferring "household help." This meant they would not live in a hotel even if it was only for a few months.

They went on to build what they called "cottages" on the grounds of the club, generally within walking distance of the main edifice. These cottages consisted of anywhere from 3,000 to 6,000 square feet, which gave them ample room to provide a domicile for their entire household staffs. Built in various styles; initially in the Victorian motif, which was in vogue. As time went by, other, more lavish styles, with a greater degree of opulence, were introduced, especially in the roaring '20s, when the club reached its zenith.

Soon after the main building was erected, they realized the members wanted more than a bedroom to occupy, so another wing was added with 8 apartments. Later they developed an annex containing 6 apartments on 3 floors and a fourth floor for household help. This building was called the Sans Souci, meaning, in French, "without care." Some of the first residents of this addition were the Morgan's, Hyde's, and Rockefeller's. Sans Souci was a misnomer when applied to these gentlemen.

In truth, the Jekyll Island Club was a great place to be employed. The majority of employees were part-timers, employed for just 3 or 4 months, and were cherry picked from prestigious establishments in the north. Staffs were more than happy to put aside all their cares, cold, snow, ice, and blizzard conditions, all travails of the frozen north. We need to remember, in that long ago time, some people were still using horses and buggies! You can only imagine what it meant to travel and luxuriate under palms, and in your off hours, to put a worm on a hook and savor the ocean and tidal basin where abundance seemed to be your right. If their northern employers gave them a problem with leaving for 3 or 4 months, usually a visit from one of the New York Union Club members could alleviate it.

The full-time staff was treated very well by the Jekyll Club superintendents and Club officers. Everything in the way of making life as pleasant as possible for the staff was provided for, including churches, medical care, out-of-the-ordinary housing, after-hour's recreation, and use of the facilities that were normally only available to the members. The golf course was a case in point: members four months, employee's *eight* months. This policy was also extended to African-Americans; Certain mores of segregation still existed here, but were trivialized to a great extent. Jekyll staff members were quite progressive for the time and locale. Surprisingly, there was very little discrimination shown, even though this Island was situated in the Deep South.

Nevertheless, even in this dreamland, certain aspects of life could not be left behind. Accidents still happened, drowning's, accidental shootings while hunting, even vehicular crashes, which seems odd given the dearth of traffic on the Island. However, most deaths occurred because of sickness, disease, or old age.

Joseph Pulitzer

One death that was particularly poignant happened to a member, "Joseph Pulitzer," held in high esteem by most members, but in others, evoked a measure of fear. He owned newspapers, namely the *New York World*, where he became the champion of the common man, with exposés and a hard-hitting, populist approach. He eventually shifted his focus to human-interest stories, scandal, and sensationalism. At one point in his career; 1909, the *World* exposed an illegal payment of $40,000,000 to the French Panama Canal Co. Pulitzer was indicted for libeling

President Theodore Roosevelt, and J. P. Morgan, the courts dismissed the indictment.

In 1887, the *World* introduced the first immensely popular comic strip in color, "The Yellow Kid." Henceforth, the term "Yellow Journalism" came into vogue and is routinely used today.

Anti-Semitism was alive and well in the country at this time, and Pulitzer was attacked in print as "Judas Pulitzer." Accolades are due the Jekyll Island Club for its forbearance of an anti-Semitic stand. If there was anti-Semitism, it was underground and only whispered in hushed tones. As a matter of fact, Pulitzer had sacked many of his friends at the club, but they never held it against him.

Pulitzer dearly loved Jekyll and generally beat the other members in taking up residence; November was his preferred time of arrival. He suffered many ailments, and as his time on this earth drew to a close, he expressed the wish that he could die at Jekyll. On October 1911, he boarded his highly prized yacht, Liberty, and in failing health, started the journey to his beloved Jekyll Island. He made it as far as Charleston Harbor, but, on October 29, he passed away, never having made it to the one spot he loved most of all.

In the voyage through life, as happens to all, "the journey is never quite complete."

∞∂∞

Creation of the Federal Reserve, November 1910

Here is truly an earth-shattering event that changed the way business was conducted in this country. Much controversy took place over this event, primarily because people felt too much power was being placed in this creation and taken away from the constitutionally-elected Congress, where the purse strings of the country were properly controlled, and given to twelve large banks, which allowed them to create money without the authorization of Congress.

In order to get this underway, it had to be done in great secrecy, so the populace would not be informed until the deed was done, fearing, if word got out, it would be squashed by Congress or a popular uprising of the people. Safety of the participants was another concern. About one third of the wealth of the world was represented there. They pulled it off smoothly, the press was never the wiser, and here is how this whole thing became reality on Jekyll Island.

Forbes magazine founder, Bertie Charles Forbes wrote several years later:

> *"Picture a party of the nation's greatest bankers stealing out of New York on a private railroad car under cover of darkness, stealthily riding hundreds of miles south, embarking on a mysterious launch, sneaking onto an island deserted by all but a few servants, living there a full week under such rigid secrecy that the names of not one of them was once mentioned, lest the servants learn the identity and disclose to the world this strangest, most secret expedition in the history of American finance.*
>
> *I am not romancing; I am giving to the world, for the first time, the real story of how the famous Aldrich currency report, the foundation of our new currency system, was written ....*
>
> *The utmost secrecy was enjoined upon all. The public must not glean a hint of what was to be done. Senator Aldrich notified each one to go quietly into a private car, of which the railroad had received orders to draw up on an unfrequented platform. Off the party set, New York's ubiquitous reporters had been foiled .... Nelson (Aldrich) had confided to Henry, Frank, Paul and Piatt that he was to keep them*

locked up at Jekyll Island, out of the rest of the world, until they had evolved and compiled a scientific currency system for the United States, the real birth of the present Federal Reserve System, the plan done on Jekyll Island in the conference with Paul, Frank and Henry .... Warburg is the link that binds the Aldrich system and the present system together. He, more than any one man, has made the system possible as a working reality."

Now, imagine if you can, the overriding reason for the Federal Reserve to exist? To keep the banks from exceeding normal boundaries and exercise due diligence when lending or investing in derivatives or other securities that may be tainted.

A short explanation of derivatives:

An investment in a security that's an intangible. Given the power the Fed has, one has to wonder where the Fed was hiding in 2007 and 2008. Not mine to question why, mine to do or die or, at the very least lose my money without whimpering.

The Federal Reserve Act was finally passed in the fall of 1913. It was based on the final edicts of Senator Nelson Aldrich, a member of the Jekyll Island Club and sponsored by Carter Glass and Robert Owen and became known as the Glass-Owen Bill.

President Woodrow and Edith Wilson

Another event of some note that took place at Jekyll Island was the visit of President Woodrow Wilson in 1915. The Club was all-atwitter over this and everyone wanted to make this a memorable stop for the highest officer of the land, so they outdid themselves.

As the President's yacht hove into view, they released an impressive display of fireworks and canon. When the President and the First Lady disembarked from a smaller sloop and stepped onto the pier, a ten-gun salute was fired by Military Reservists obtained from Brunswick, Georgia. Appropriate Flags and Bunting lined the path to the Club. It was a gala affair in the dining room and ballroom that evening. Waltzes by a string quartet gave just the right tone to the whole event. Edith Galt Wilson, the First Lady, was at first prepared to be bored on one of the innumerable trips required of sitting Presidents. Once she was mesmerized by the paradigm of an example that existed only on this Island, and was wined, dined and feted by the extraordinary gentleman of this very unique club, her attitude did a complete turnaround. That evening was one, in later years, she would reminisce about.

∞∂∞

Winners and Losers

World War I was now underway in Europe, and our country was entering a period of deep concern for our boys, who would be embarking for the continent and dying in some God forsaken foxhole or trench. It would be a long time before we, as a nation would rise with our heads up and see a brighter future. World War II would be the final cataclysmic event that would write the last chapter of the Jekyll Island Club.

The many good things that happened at this club were interspersed with tragedy, but none more tragic then the eventual demise of the life and times of not only this club, but of America. The 1920s was truly the time to be a member of Jekyll. The financial markets were soaring and businesses were roaring. After all, it was called "The Roaring '20s" and everybody had untold resources. Credit was readily available, securities were bought with 10% down on the dollar and millionaires were literally made overnight. President Hoover proclaimed "two chickens in every pot, two cars in every garage." People partied away the night doing the dances of the age, the Charleston, the Big Apple, the Black Bottom, Jitterbug was now making an appearance, woman were smoking in public and styles that woman wore enhanced sexuality.

Finally, 1929 came and the party was over. It came to an end with a crash and a gigantic hangover as most parties do. The club began to reel under the crushing weight of expenses and declining memberships. Former millionaires were going into bankruptcy and literally walking out on their beautiful Jekyll Island homes, totally abandoning them, and taking nothing, leaving even their furniture behind.

The club cast about in desperation for ways to save itself. Memberships were expanded and fees lowered, which was self-defeating, because there were no members to be found at any price.

Whenever you think things cannot get any worse, of course they will. A double whammy hit and World War II became a reality. All of our industry converted to war materials. Ford,

General Motors, and others were now making tanks. Henry Kaiser was building Liberty Ships and became known for his fast production methods. Rationing was the rage. Whenever you saw a line forming, you got in it, and whatever they were providing, you needed it.

The most critical shortage was men. The draft sucked away most of the men, depleting the labor supply. This put the final nail in the coffin of the Jekyll Club, and after heroic efforts to keep the Club alive, it was closed at the end of the 1942 season. There was a glimmer of hope that the Club would become viable again after the war, but this hope faded and the Club became a ward of the State of Georgia in 1947, when the entire island was purchased by the State Government.

The state tried operating the entire complex as a resort, but, financially, it was a failure and closed again in 1971. It was designated as an historic landmark in 1978.

The 1930's sucked the life out of, not only The Jekyll Island Club, but the country too. If we include inflation, it took 40 years just to return to where we were financially in 1929.

As sad as it is to think about the demise of this picturesque and exquisite piece of history, there is an upside to this continuing story. We must remember this had been a place that the average person would never get to see, and to walk about the magic of its tree-lined lanes, or rent a bike and cruise around as they did in 1898. Now, that is possible because of its latest reincarnation as a luxury resort hotel. Restoration was begun in 1985 and it was reopened as an opulent resort.

If you desire to return for a brief moment to the past, then grab your suitcase and your credit card or checkbook and shuffle off to Jekyll Island.

Jesse Livermore
The Great Bear of Wall Street

At the end of this chapter, I will reveal the secret that was the source of Jesse Livermore earning many millions in the stock market and the mystery that contributed to his eventual demise.

Jesse Livermore. That name will live in the annals of fame wherever men of intellect gather to discuss investments and winning and losing on that great street called Wall Street, names that can be mentioned in the same breath, Bernard Baruch, J. P. Morgan, Billy Durant, John D. Rockefeller, Joe Kennedy, Richard Whitney and many others that became legendary.

Most of the great speculators made much of their fortunes from the bull market of the 1920s. We came to refer to that time as the Roaring '20s. A time that, for many of us, held a fascination because of America breaking away from a traditionalist and conservative way of life to an avant-garde lifestyle. It was the heyday of prohibition, speakeasies, gangsters, flappers, dances that were fast and provocative like the Charleston, the Black Bottom, the Big Apple, the beginning of the Jitterbug.

Women were suddenly free to become a part of life they never before experienced. They now smoked in the open, drank booze in the open, adhered to contemporary styles of dress that clearly showed a new sexuality, with hairstyles that were a significant departure from the past.

The Start of the Great Depression

On black Thursday, October 24, 1929, the stock market started falling precipitously at the opening bell. This was the clarion call for the bankers, and movers and shakers to hold a meeting and essentially do what they formerly did to stop a market panic in 1907. The meeting included, Thomas W. Lamont, acting head of Morgan Bank; Albert Wiggin, head of the Chase National Bank and Charles G. Mitchell, President of the National City Bank of New York. Richard Whitney, Vice President of the New York Exchange, who later would become president of the Exchange, and end up in prison for misappropriation. A nice word for embezzlement. Richard became the front man for this illustrious group, the man they forgot about and the one that was the driving force in the 1907 debacle of the securities market was *Jesse Livermore*. Jesse was involved in selling prodigious amounts of stock short, a powerful mechanism for driving stock prices down. It involved borrowing shares and selling them immediately with the intention of buying the security back at some future date and replacing it at a lower price. Of course, this just fed upon itself. The more it went down the more sellers entered the market and the more it went down. And round and round it went.

October 29, 1929, **Black Tuesday**
The day the Roaring '20s ended.

Winners and Losers

On this day, the market sank into a black hole and set a new record for number of shares traded. It also portended the birth of the Great Depression.

At this point, I believe I must explain in more detail what a short sale is. It occurs when a speculator borrows stock from his broker and immediately sells it to take advantage of the current price and hopefully buy it back at a lower price, and replace the shares that he borrowed. Let's say that GM stock is selling at 100 and the speculator believes that GM stock will decline. He will borrow the number of shares that he wants to sell and get the price that it is selling at currently. If GM declines to 90 or any amount below the price he sold it at, he can buy it back and replace the borrowed stock. At $90, he will make a ten-dollar profit. Let's further assume that margin is 10-percent, which means he borrows 90-percent, and let me interject here, a 10-percent margin is not in the cards in the present day. Currently it is 50-percent. Now, he sells 1000 shares, and the cost of shares if he had bought them would have been $100,000. But he needed to put up only $10,000. If he made a return of $10 a share, his profit is $10,000 or a percentage return of 100%. If you can understand all that, you are now an expert and can now make millions in the market.

Of course, I was being facetious, but can you see why many people felt that way? You watched your neighbor scrape together $1000 and make three or four thousand before the month was out, not by selling short but buying long. Long in this context meant actually buying and owning a security. There was a general feeling at that time that the market had reached a new level and would only go up from here. This Pollyanna view was promoted by reporters, pseudo financial experts and other market pundits of the day. History does repeat itself. Haven't we heard the siren song of that old refrain just about every time we are in an exalted bull market? Of course, the lemmings enter at about this time and guess who ends up on the short end of the stick?

In the foregoing, I refer to the lemmings as the small, uninformed investor, but Jesse was not just a prolific short seller; he simply went with the market. By tape reading, he could divine whether the market, in its entirety, was headed in an upward or downward direction. Once that was determined, then, and only then, he would select a stock and either bet it short or long. By looking closely at the volume and momentum of a security, he could tell in many cases which way the momentum of the issue was headed.

We must remember his trading system was not as simplified as the foregoing indicates. Many long hours and days and years were involved in the building of Jesse's system. By getting a feel for this 1929 market during the course of the year, he determined that it was vastly overpriced. During the summer, he started shorting the market, but the securities he shorted kept going up, which of course was the wrong direction. If Jesse had one virtue, it was patience. He was absolutely positive this market was overpriced, and it was just a matter of time before the break came. Come it did ... with a vengeance. It is generally believed that the selling climaxed on October 29 when new records of volume were set. However the securities markets continued down until the Second World War started, a total of about 10 years. Taking inflation into consideration, it took a total of 40 years for the market to get back to where it was at its height in the fateful year of 1929.

Shorting the market in this horrendous period of time, Jesse reached the peak of his life as far as his fortune was concerned. He earned in 1929 approximately 100 million dollars of course, you can only imagine what that meant during the 30's.

Yes, the Roaring Twenties ended, but with a roaring, unimaginable crash that hopefully we will never see again. A philosopher once said, *"If we forget history, we are doomed to*

Winners and Losers

repeat it." This, then, was a time of suicides. It was widely reported that men were jumping out of high-rise buildings. It was also a time of soup lines, men, women and children, living on the street, or in bushes, or abandoned buildings, or patched tents and ramshackle structures put together with grocery boxes that at one time held oranges or apples. People were begging for anything they could get, food, money, a job, whatever was offered. The poverty and suffering was unimaginable and it extended to the entire U. S.

Farmers actually were hit with this downturn more than the city dwellers, hit with a double whammy when the great dust storms came along in the '30s, and the massive migration to California and the western U. S. began. Have you ever heard of the term Okies? That's what they were called. Hatred was rampant among the permanent residents they were displacing. One can only imagine the despair they were all feeling.

Jesse was the most hated man on Wall Street, because of his predilection of selling stocks which tended to drive the market in the wrong direction, *down*. This sentiment included President Herbert Hoover; whom the populace put the blame on for the Great Depression.

It therefore became incumbent on Jesse to protect his family. Answering his phone was not an option, because of the venom that was spewed out when he did answer it. Bodyguards were hired to protect his wife and children, and various mansions that contained many beautiful antiques, paintings and other possessions, were closely guarded.

Jesse started at the tender age of 14 as a chalkboard boy, in a firm called Paine Webber. This came about after he ran away from home, but with the encouragement of his mother, who realized he did not belong on a hardscrabble farm etching a living out of an unforgiving, stone-filled patch of dirt.

Jesse was an exceedingly bright young man with a penchant for mathematics. Having landed this job as a chalkboard boy, he undoubtedly felt it was the job of his dreams. He loved being involved in the chaotic and frenzied action on "the floor." The constant hammering of the ticker tape, the brokers yelling out orders, the names of the companies on the board, with changing numbers every second, men winning and losing thousands of dollars in every change of the numbers was like candy to young Jesse and his appetite for it knew no bounds.

The things he learned there would stand him in good stead in later years, the basis for the system of trading he eventually developed. It was called "tape reading," in other words, getting a feel for the market or a particular stock. He began to realize that these numbers ran in a pattern and could be predictable. His affinity for numbers would be the basis for his ability to accumulate the many millions of dollars this talent created for him.

You would think that with his keen, mathematical background, he would have a conservative bent, but that wasn't the case at all. He was a plunger, and he became known as the "boy plunger of Wall Street." This led to his being broke, losing everything he had, not once, not twice, but many times. In fact, so many times he lost track.

So, you see, it wasn't the money, like many of the outstanding men and women of our time, and in times past, it was "the game," the money only a way of knowing if you were winning or losing.

Panic of 1907

The panic of 1907 was a loan driven, market downturn. Every day at noon bankers would appear at the posts of the Stock Exchange and announce to the brokers how much call money they had to offer. Call money was the funds that the brokers made available to their customers so they would have margin to buy stocks. This was the grease that made the brokers and some customers wealthy. The banks suddenly ran out of money. This happened because the brokers had become overextended.

If money was not obtainable, then it follows that the amount of stock sold and bartered on the exchange would show a precipitous decline. Hence, a crash would be in the offing. Then, as now, everybody needed the availability of liquid money from sources that supplied the loans, banks, insurance companies, etc. This was one of the factors that contributed to every crash that we have experienced in our history, including our recent steep declines, i.e. 1987 and 2008.

The question becomes; do we currently have circuit breakers in place to blunt a steep decline in the market? That is worrisome, considering the speed of trading in our modern, electronically-driven era.

Back in 1907, a market decline would be blunted by a consortium of immensely wealthy men and entities, which would supply enough muscle, and by that I mean, money to start buying stocks in enough volume to halt the decline. That tactic can't work today. The sheer size of our interconnected markets would preclude this particular method from being effective.

J. P. Morgan

When it came to the attention of J. P. Morgan that a problem was developing in the market, he sent one of his men to the exchange to tell them that call money would be there at the opening of the market. He summoned the banks and ordered them to make call money available immediately. When they asked where they would get the money, he replied, "They should raid their reserves." The banks replied, "We will be in violation of banking codes." Morgan said, "I'll personally guarantee your reserves. More than that, he gathered many of the most powerful men in the country to start buying some of the most high-profile stocks.

J. P., being a wise man, knew what most people on Wall Street did not, that Jesse Livermore would be the most prolific short seller on the street, contributing to the sliding prices of stocks. He knew, that in order to halt the slippery slope, he must enlist his participation. With all due swiftness, he sent an emissary to speak to J. L. as he liked to be called. Jesse had never been sought out by a man as powerful as J. P. Morgan, and he was duly flattered. Jesse did not have an ego and did not consider himself as having much in the way of power in the overall market, but he quickly complied when Morgan asked him to curtail operations.

The next morning, he immediately covered his shorts, went long in some high volume companies and the panic of 1907 was averted. However, his intervention by going long in the market cost Jesse dearly. This then, was the thing that made him strengthen his resolve. He would never again listen to another person, or be overcome and impressed by another's fame or importance.

Never take a tip or insider information. Never let his ego interfere with the business of making money. Always go it alone. These were his credos, but, because of human frailty, he did violate this rule once or twice, and each time, it cost him lost time and money.

Jesse was the personification of the Roaring 20's. Slim, blond, pale blue eyes, very much a meticulous dresser, he had a tendency to be flamboyant. He had several mansions properly staffed with butlers and maids, not to mention yachts that reached upwards of 300 feet and properly staffed. This was in keeping with his personality. Everything about him was orderly and neat, something that extended into his entire life. He arose at the same time, ate at the same time, and had his chauffeur and Rolls Royce bring him to his palatial and regal office at the same time. Order did not always extend to trading activities. He was primarily a tape reader; however, he could be impetuous and spontaneous. He never took, or listened to, tips or inside information. The few times he did, had disastrous consequences.

One particular occurrence did not meet with an undue loss of capital. It seems Jesse had an unreal clairvoyance and feel for things that might happen in the future that would have an effect on his trading. For instance, he decided to sell short Union Pacific Railroad for no known reason, two days before the disastrous San Francisco earthquake hit, and literally made him a fortune when the bottom fell out of Union Pacific stock.

The following is the one time that J. L. did not follow his rules of the game, much to his chagrin, and it led to his eventual bankruptcy. On one of Jesse's many excursions to Palm

Beach, which he found wondrous in the richness of its population, the beauty of its mansions and the verdant nature of its environs, he was enjoying himself in the exquisite confines of the most celebrated casino of its day, called Bradley's Beach Club. Sitting at the bar, with Lillian Russell, the most alluring actress and singer of the day, and Edward Bradley, the proprietor of the establishment, a gentleman by the name of Percy Thomas entered. Known as the cotton king, it was a well-known fact he had a wealth of knowledge in the commodities market. Suave, smooth, self-assured and a persona that could only be called enigmatic, he was the complete opposite of J. L. Where Jesse tended to be withdrawn and taciturn, Thomas was open, loquacious, and personable.

Jesse operated alone, without inside information or, many times, without any information at all. Remember, he was a tape reader and acted only on the information the tape gave him. But Percy had an all-encompassing knowledge and many spies working for him. He had acquired, through the force of his personality, many people who were in positions to enable him to acquire knowledge of privileged situations. Only after his information was complete, would he purchase a position in that particular investment.

J. L. and Percy eventually established an exceptionally close bond and Jesse started believing that the way Percy speculated was the perfect way to trade. One time in the past the cotton king had gone broke. Jesse always had the ability to coldly analyze any situation and now this happenstance weighed on Jesse's mind. How could Percy go broke if he knew everything?

Regardless of his haunting suspicions, Jesse was eventually hooked. He had an uncommonly bright, inquiring mind and all of the frailties of a human being. He thought there was always a better way to do things. All of the lessons he had learned in many years of trading were put aside. This had to be a better way because all the information that Percy had accumulated said so. Yet, he forgot the most powerful lesson of all. *The market seldom does what you think it ought to do.*

The other valuable lesson? *Trade by yourself and keep your own counsel.* Jesse was now playing another man's game and it was a time of impending disasters that meant bankruptcy for Jesse.

Lillian Russell

Diamond Jim Brady

Lillian Russell was the first to go. He found her high maintenance ways too rich for his new position in life, so he sent her back to Diamond Jim Brady, a former companion of hers. He was an extremely corpulent man, who had a fascination for diamonds and could well afford them. Owning and doing many things, Diamond Jim was a successful and controversial businessman, known to be somewhat unethical. We're not sure if Diamond Jim knew that Lillian was spending time with other men, or if he even cared. Lillian believed the size of a man's waist was of no concern, but the size of his wallet was immensely influential to her.

Anita Venetian

Jesse's mansion in New York

The second thing to go was his yacht, his beloved *Anita Venetian*, and one by one, the estates were liquidated and he pawned the many jewels' his wife had accumulated.

Jesse was now back in an environment that he was all too familiar with. Slammed to earth with a thud that made waves throughout Wall Street and with hat in hand, J. L. went visiting all of the old brokers he had done business with in the past. They had persevered with him in other times, and this time was no different. They rushed to his side and made margin available to him so he could start trading again and it did not take long for Jesse to start acquiring his former status.

There was a price to be paid, however. A hole was left in Jesse's persona. Some of the cocksure stride was gone, and many times, he found himself trading without conviction. This hampered his formula for success and increased his many moods of depression. Possibly, he became bipolar or manic-depressive. This condition would last the rest of his life. He was not getting the pleasure that he had previously experienced in the times when he was winning large amounts of money.

Ziegfeld Follies—Jesse's wife—Dorothy

The one thing that stayed with him was his attraction for the opposite sex. He for them and them for him. Always a handsome man, he loved beautiful ladies. As a matter of fact, F. Scott Fitzgerald, who created the phrase The Roaring Twenties, probably used Jesse as his model for Gatsby when writing his best-selling, wildly popular book, *The Great Gatsby*. I believe that Fitzgerald and J. L. were friends and had been to many of the parties that Jesse's Ziegfeld Follies second wife, Dorothy, sponsored. Both Fitzgerald and Dorothy were alcoholics, so there was somewhat of a bond infused into this relationship.

The drinking and loose morals of the rich and famous, or infamous, whichever way you want to term it, was the beginning of the final chapter of the Jesse Livermore saga. Here, the degradation and dissipation take place. It is difficult to pin the entire blame on either party. Certainly, there was enough to go around. Jesse had his amorous ways and thirst for beautiful showgirls. Dorothy had her thirst for the demon rum. This led Dorothy to have numerous affairs, especially since she was living with a man who spent most of his time being morose and in a deep dark funk and seemingly did not care about his wife or children. He, however had to come home to an alcoholic and those of you who ever had to live with a person whose only reason for living was to get to the next drink, know how absolutely disgusting this can be and how repulsive they are in their personal habits and with alcoholic friends swarming around them.

When they divorced in 1932, I believe it was the end for Jesse. He still carried a torch for her, but they just could not be together. She knew of his extra-marital affairs, and that tore at her heart. Of course, she started having her own dalliances and eventually a nasty split took place over the children. She eventually won custody, and J. L. took it hard. It was difficult for him to understand how two very privileged boys could be brought up in an atmosphere of alcoholism.

He did provide her with a generous settlement as he did with his first wife. Believing he would make it up in a short while, as he was able to do all of his life. A short list of what he gave her follows:

- A one million dollar portfolio of stocks hand-picked by Jesse,
- A beautiful awe-inspiring estate that was the envy of her many friends and was used by Fitzgerald as the model of the mansion in his book The Great Gatsby
- All the exquisite furnishings, including Louie the XIV furnishings
- Tons of silverware, including the Napoleon serving set for sixteen.
- Several beautiful cars, including a Rolls Royce.
- Persian rugs.
- Drapes and window dressings that Scarlet O'Hara would have married Rhett for.
- The interior of the mansion had been appointed by the exceptional decorators of the day.

Winners and Losers

After the divorce in the courthouse, she immediately walked into another courtroom and married a man by the name of Walter Longcope, a tax collector, a handsome man, but who certainly had never known money like Dorothy had. This too ended in divorce.

The first thing that left Dorothy's possession was Jesse's handpicked stock portfolio. Under the advice of a Financial Advisor of the day, who told her that railroad bonds with their attractive dividends would give her a lovely annual income? This is the same advice that we receive from present day Advisors, whose mantra is mutual funds, bonds, or annuities. Eventually, her railroad bonds became worthless. If she had kept the handpicked portfolio by J. L., it would have been worth 50 million by 1950.

She eventually moved into the mansion *Evermore*. She took her two dogs with her, and while she lolled around in a drunken haze, she never took the dogs out onto the expansive and expensive grounds. They proceeded to urinate and defecate on the beautiful Persian rugs, and when the rugs were too foul and the stench unbearable, she just rolled them up and threw them out.

The Louie XIV furniture was so badly mistreated, to say they were junk would have been upgrading them to an unattainable status. When the taxman presented her a bill on the home, she sent it on to Jesse, which he promptly ignored and the home was foreclosed on.

The cost of the antique furniture was in the millions. The home was appraised in 1932 at $1,350,000, the landscaping at $150,000, the silverware at $100,000, a Rolls Royce at $22,000 and jade ornaments at $300,000. The entire ensemble, auctioned, hammer down at $250,000.

Jesse remarried eight months later to a socialite, Harriet Metz Noble of Omaha, Nebraska, from a wealthy family that owned the Metz Brewery in Omaha. Harriet was an Opera singer and with her résumé came a truly ominous sign. This shows the depths that the once well-respected speculator had reached. She had been married four previous times. That's bad enough, but can you imagine a man, reputed to have a brilliant mind, after what he had been through, marrying a woman who's four previous husbands committed suicide. "Whoa, wait a minute!" Jesse should have given this more than a passing thought.

I believe that this woman was a very controlling person and Jesse was at a point in his life that existence held no interest for him. In other words, he allowed her to dictate his life and he proceeded to follow her around like a little puppy dog. This was so unlike Jesse. No longer did vivacity and excitement exist in his way of life. Events would later occur that were catastrophic to Jesse.

He hardly saw his two boys, Jesse, Jr. and Paul anymore because they were off at school and Dorothy's hatred for J. L. made it difficult for him to see them. Nevertheless, he loved them with all of his heart. He may not have physically seen them, but Daddy was always there when they needed anything. The one thing they needed more than anything else was his presence and counsel, something which he was incapable of giving.

Jesse Jr. a young man who was endowed with the good looks of his parents, was now becoming a problem for Dorothy, as many of her erstwhile lady friends became enamored of his looks and charms, though they were much older. They found having an afternoon tryst with this attractive young man enticing, and of course, he liked what alcohol did to him. Paul, the younger son, was certainly more sober in his appreciation of life and eventually had a small career in movies.

An evening when all combatants were inebriated, Jesse, Jr. started having a heated argument with his mother, probably over any number of things that people in their cups insanely argue about. Junior ran upstairs to grab a rifle, brought it downstairs to his mother, and handed it to her.

"You always wanted to do this," he said, "so here is your chance, shoot me."

Dorothy, in a drunken stupor, took him up on his challenge and pulled the trigger on a rifle that she thought was just a ruse. What she thought was an empty weapon, fired, and hit Jesse in the chest. In slurred words, she started screaming.

"Oh, my God! I've shot my son!" she cried, over and over again.

She eventually collapsed on the floor. Other people who were there called an ambulance and Jesse Jr., still alive, was taken to the emergency room. J. L. was promptly notified and rushed to the hospital where, upon seeing his son grabbed his hand.

"Fight, Jess, fight as hard as you can!" he said in despair.

And fight he did, eventually surviving this traumatic event, after many prayers from J. L. and Dorothy.

The bitterness deepened between the two of them, but, when J. L. walked away, he knew the time he would spend with his family was growing short. He was already planning his final exit.

Everything was finalizing, all of the various lawsuits that were happening. His ex-wife was suing him for the hospital bills that they were charging for his son. The Federal Government was suing for back taxes. Other people were suing just to get a piece of the fast disappearing fortune that was left, any spare change that they could get their grimy gritty hands on. These were the vultures that appeared whenever someone was down, and they thought an opportunity to feed on the bones of a decaying carcass presented itself.

Jesse was now incapable of trading like days of yore. Depression had completely engulfed him. For so many years, all of his adult life, the only thing he knew, the stock market, was now useless to him. He felt no need to go on living. Death would be a welcome respite from the terrible pain he now felt every waking moment.

J. L. and his son Paul did collaborate on a book in 1940 called, *How to Trade in Stocks*. This was an exercise in futility. At this time, J. L. certainly had remarkably little idea of how to trade in stocks, and the book sold inadequately. It has become more popular now than it was then.

On Wednesday November 27, 1940, Jesse and his wife went to one of their favorite places, the Stork Club. Jesse only picked at his food and seemed rather distant, with a faraway look in his eye. His wife, Harriet asked if there was anything wrong. He replied, he had a feeling of tiredness, so they made their goodbyes to their friend, Sherman Billingsley the owner of the Stork Club, and departed rather early.

**Jesse and second wife Harriet at the Stork Club…
He committed suicide the next day**

The next morning, on Thursday November 28, 1940, J. L. went to his office in the Squibb Building as usual and later left to go to the Sherry Netherland Hotel. He had at one time lived here and still knew a few people. It was customary for Jesse to stop here and have a cocktail when leaving his office for the day. He briefly talked to the manager and then walked into the bar, where the bartender made his usual Old Fashioned.

As he sat having lunch, he occasionally entered something on a small pad and then placed it in his pocket. The bartender thought he seemed distraught and uptight. He finally rose from the table and walked toward the banquet area and then to a cloakroom just off the ballroom. He sat on a stool, pulled a .32-cal. automatic from his pocket, calmly shot himself behind his right ear and died instantly. The notes on the pad in his pocket, as disclosed by the police, took the form of a suicide note:

My dear Nina; Things have gotten bad with me. I'm tired of fighting. Can't carry on any longer. This is the only way out. I am unworthy of your love. I am a failure. I am truly sorry, but this is the only way out for me.

There may have been more to his last words, but nothing further was ever disclosed.

∞∂∞

The crassness of people never ceases to amaze me. Jesse's son Paul hurried over to Jesse's home to give some solace to the new widow. She apparently didn't need it. She was too busy carrying out bags full of money that Jesse kept in the apartment to foil the many people that had designs on what was left of his wealth. As Paul watched, she went to the safe and scraped out the many jewels they had accumulated, carried them out to the waiting chauffer, and made her goodbyes to Paul.

And so ended a life that had everything: intelligence, richness, many friends, loves, success, fame, and failure. What a shame it ended as it did, the life of one of the last men to have experienced the thrill of the *Gilded Age*.

As I wrote this chapter, I felt deeply the emptiness of its ending and the termination of this special life. Only one question remains. *Why?*

Ron Chicone

Trading Secrets of Jesse Lauriston Livermore

My own experience in trading securities rivals Jesse's in the length of time that I spent in the business. I learned to read financial pages of the newspaper at about nine years old. My father, an immigrant from Italy, only had a fourth grade education. The inability to speak English with any degree of clarity was the reason he was still in the fourth grade when he quit school to go to work. Living in Hubbard, Ohio, there seemed to be a plethora of jobs in the steel industry. He lied about his age, but, in those days, that was not a problem. If you were big enough, and willing to hold up your end of the job in the blast furnaces, your employers were happy and would not challenge your age credentials. During that time period, this was a horrendous job, since they had none of the safety precautions that are common today.

My father's belief in the American system grew stronger as time went on. Yes, he did suffer through the depression and I was old enough to remember when he had to go on relief simply to provide for the family. The men in the family would get up in the dark of the night to go to the train yards where they would hope to find coal that had fallen from the trains as they passed, and they were not above giving the coal a little help in falling from the coal cars.

At that time, the railroads employed security guards that were instructed to shoot at people who dared to breach the confines of the railroad yards. I don't know if they meant to shoot directly at them or just enough to scare the bee-*jesses* out of them. They were given the popular name, *Son-of- a- Bitch Railroad Dicks*.

To keep the lights on in our home, meant working for the utility company four days a month. Many times working sixteen hours a day. The mode of transportation to and from work was open dump trucks regardless of the weather.

Winners and Losers

The Roosevelt administration eventually started a program called the Works Progress Administration, or WPA for short, and halleluiah, my father had a job. Not much of one, but one in which you went to work every day. The ability to use a shovel was the main requirement to work on the WPA and they even paid you; not much, but, by God, it was a paycheck.

Times did get better when my father was able to land a job with General Motors. That's where the realization that he could become an owner of the company by buying stock on the stock exchange took place. His experience working for General Motors gave him the belief that this company would become richer as time went on. My dad became a part of the American dream by becoming a stockholder in the General Motors Company.

Because I showed an interest in stocks, he let me tag along with his excursions to a Paine Webber or a Merrill Lynch brokerage office. These were located on the public square in Youngstown, Ohio. Time has dimmed my memory somewhat, but I, like Jesse, was fascinated by the big board and the flashing numbers and symbols. My father, formerly a language handicapped immigrant, eventually taught me the rudiments of reading the financial pages. In time I became a Financial Advisor and retired after a career of over 30 years.

Now, following that long soliloquy, we finally come to the reason I might have a unique ability to analyze the trading systems of Jesse Livermore. First of all, is Jesse's system out of date? Not by a long shot, the difference is his approach to trading has come into the mainstream. What he called tape reading, we call charting. What took him hours or days to divine from tape reading, we do in a matter of seconds with computers. Insider trading is given to us almost immediately; what would have taken days to determine back then. News on a security is generally instantaneous, but not always. In this day and age, our tape is always running current, not lagging behind. Sometimes it was hours behind in Jesse's day.

To get an execution on one's trade in today's world is a matter of a few seconds. The cost of making a trade is much less today, hence the advent of the day trader. That would have been anathema in Jesse's day because of costs involved. Yet, the basic premise is still the same:

1) Determine the momentum of the general securities market. There are three kinds of movements that involve securities, Up, Down, Sideways.

2) Make a determination of the sectors that are reacting in the same direction as the general market.

3) Make a determination of the securities that are reacting in the same direction as the general market.

4) If a market is going in a sideways direction, Jesse would generally stay out of the market unless the tapes would be indicating through the volume and chart/tape pattern, that a general turn in this security was indicated.

5) Never take advice from other people.

6) Never yield to insider information

7) Do yourself a favor and be a lone wolf.

8) Volume, volume, volume, was Jesse's big obsession and for an excellent reason.

9) Volume was able to tell Jesse if a security was going up or down or getting ready for a transitional turn.

10) Remember, the market is more of an art than a science.

11) Learning to have a feel for the market, or security, is of overriding importance.

12) As you mature in your trading methods, volume will become more important to you and to your ability to beat the market.

Examples:
a) Stock that is riding higher on decreasing volume is probably going to start trending the other way, or getting ready to stagnate.
b) Stock that is trending higher on incremental increases in volume will, in all likelihood, go higher.
c) The reverse may be true. A stock that is going lower on incremental increases in volume is more likely going to go lower.
d) Here is the catch. If a security has a sudden spike along with an increase in volume, either up or down in its trend, then that is what is called an exhaustion spike, or peak, and that security will now generally take a turn either up or down. The reason is that it has exhausted either the buyers or sellers in that security.
e) Notice that, in all cases, I have referred to the various different movements in a security with a connotation such as, generally, more than likely, probably, likelihood, or maybe. The reason is, the market has a peculiar way of reacting and having a mind of its own. Jesse only tried to put the prevailing odds in his favor.

13) Remember, being right all the time is impossible. The goal is being right 60% of the time.

14) Jesse, in most cases, liked to test a security before making a decisive move and he would invest small amounts. If the investment moved in the proper direction with strength, meaning volume and satisfactory movement of the price, either up or down, it would finally give him the conviction that he was correct in his assessment of that investment and he now would make a much larger outlay of capital.

15) Never allow a loss of greater than 10%. A favorite homily of mine that falls in the same category: Never fall in love with any investment because it will never love you back.

16) Absolutely do not listen to other investors that will try to tell you how truly great they are doing in the market. Always treat them as prevaricators and never allow dreams of sugarplums to dance in your head.

I must give my impressions of the real reason that Jesse eventually failed in the final days of his career. Of course I will also point out that many other successful traders failed in the '30s. Why, all of a sudden, did nothing go right for them? It was because of the quirky nature of the market in that period of time. Their previous experiences taught them that markets always righted themselves. That had been so right through most of the time there were security markets.

I'm sure you have heard of long term investing? Keeping and holding quality stocks over the long term. There are many market mavens who espouse that same rhetoric today, and mostly, they are right. But, occasionally, they are wrong with disaster lurking around the corner. This is where Jesse's 10% rule came into play. When a stock went against him ten percent, he would cover his positions, and terminate that investment.

What most traders could not understand was, how could a market go down for ten years? Human frailty rears its ugly head and says it must go up, so they kept investing. This is called averaging down. They should have been standing on the sidelines looking and waiting. They made their living from the market in years gone by. That was no longer available to them. Their living expenses were high, and they never realized, until it was too late, that the game was over.

Jesse's problem, when he invested long, was the market went sideways or advanced in small increments and he made no money. When he invested short, the market went sideways, or if it did go in the direction he expected, it was not enough to cover his exorbitant expenses and the debits continued to pile up. Jesse's mental health kept deteriorating, coupled to the pressure of staving off bankruptcy once again. Add to that his much older age, the many lawsuits he was facing and the pain that his life held.

Those of you who have experienced depression know the anguish of it. Life no longer held a fascination for him, and he could not carry on. As he wrote in his suicide note, it was incumbent upon him to end it.

Consider this: there are many excuses for failure, but none for success.

The securities market is an art, not a science.

A Great American Institution

[*Featuring, John Jack Bradley and Steve Juliano, who helped immeasurably in the writing of this Chapter.*]

In this Chapter it is not my intention to eulogize individuals that I have highlighted, I have used them to bring to your attention the inner feel and importance of horse racing as it had such an important role in our country and the world. If you can use the phrase winners and losers, then that is what horse racing is all about. It has a majesty all its own. Ask any King and Queen, or Head of State. That is why it has been called the Sport of Kings.

The most exciting two minutes in all of sports, that is what they call the Kentucky Derby. I wholeheartedly agree. I believe I have never watched a race that did not give me a thrill. However, this race and its adjuncts, Pimlico and The Belmont that comprise The Triple Crown are so unique and famous, no matter where one goes in this world, all you have to say is "The Derby" or "The Triple Crown", and everyone knows the races you are referring to.

Man-O-War

Secretariat

The names of the "Legendary Horses" that have competed in these events ring in my ears every time someone mentions the Kentucky Derby. To wit: War Admiral, Assault, Citation, Affirmed, Spectacular Bid and one of the greatest horses of all time, Secretariat, along with a thoroughbred called Man-O-War, who never won the Derby because he was never entered, but his name has to be included whenever great horses of all time are mentioned. (As an aside: Man-O-War won 20 of 21 races. He lost while racing in the mud to a colt named Upset.)

As a young boy, I spent most of my summers at my grandmother's in a section called Briarhill, in Youngstown, Ohio. I must say that they were idyllic. When I think back, it was Huckleberry Finn time, a time in the past when organized activities for children were nonexistent. Therefore, every day was a spontaneous adventure that we would create. Our elders were not concerned for our whereabouts unless we were late for dinner. Crime, at least in our neighborhood, did not exist.

Those of you who know Youngstown and are familiar of its past reputation as crime infested would be surprised to learn, in our area, we went everywhere with nary a thought for our safety. One of my best friends as a youngster was a tough little kid with tight curly hair and blue eyes who lived down the street and around the corner. To describe that kid as tough meant, if someone was going to be in a disagreement with him and it would come to blows, no matter how big the opponent, it would behoove that person to bring his lunch, because he was going to be there for a while. This kid taught me the meaning of perseverance. His real interest in life was an all-consuming interest in horseracing. Yes, that was the beginning of my degenerate ways concerning the racetrack.

A mystifying thing for most people at the track is what they euphemistically call the racing form, which is the past performance of all the horses racing that day. Now, if a person is not a connoisseur of racing, and inadvertently ran across one of these things, he would come to the realization that all horseplayers who read and understand the racing form can be considered geniuses. Well, my buddy taught me to read the form when I was about ten or eleven years old. Now, that is what I call a friend and he probably cost me many thousands of coin of the realm over the years. May I say it was worth it, the experiences, priceless. I do want to relate, one of the experiences, or should I say adventures that certainly could have come from a modern day Huck Finn.

We lived about seventy-five miles from a racetrack in Cleveland called Randall Park, which is now a shopping center. In talking to my friend, a young man called Nick Lasko, we hatched the idea that we could hitchhike there and back in one day. I believe that we were about eleven or twelve when this idea hit us, certainly no older, because, by 13, we had gained some modicum of wisdom and at that advanced age, would not have considered such a hare-brained scheme.

Winners and Losers

Randall Park

Early one morning, the things needed for the trip were trotted out. In our case, it consisted of the clothes we were wearing. Of course, we forgot to take our brains along, which was natural considering our immaturity at the time.

I said to Nick, "How about food?"

"Don't worry about it," he said. "Somebody will give us something to eat when we get into the track."

His supreme confidence made my questioning seem parochial, but, by this time, some element of common sense was creeping into my head and I was having reservations about our little caper... "Hey, wait a minute, Nick. Don't they have a fence around the whole track?"

"Not to worry, remember how we managed to get through Old Farmer Jim's fence when we were stealing his apples?"

"Yes, but when we were desperately leaving and Old Jim was chasing us with a pitchfork, it did not take much to clear that fence. Remember, it was only about six feet high. At that time, I was so scared I could have roared right through it."

I know now that Farmer Jim used that pitchfork to render us with an inability to try that adventure again and it worked. We never went back to partake of those apples.

"And how about all the times we went either over, or under, the fence at the high school football games?"

"Yeah Nick, remember, the cop on duty was nice enough to look the other way when we were going over the fence or under it, as the case may be."

I guess he took pity on those street urchins who did not have the wherewithal to enter at the turnstiles. Of course, we were only following tradition; all of our friends were doing the same thing. Well, Nick in his superior wisdom seemed so confident and sure of himself that it did a lot to buck up my flagging spirits.

It just so happens that route 422 used to go right through the neighborhood, and that was a straight shot to the racetrack. As luck would have it, we were able to get a ride almost immediately and went straight to the track. One would have thought that motorists would think it strange two young kids were hitchhiking. However, that was not the case, because, in that long ago age of my childhood, it was the preferred mode of transportation. Now, to the next problem of getting in.

"No problem." Nick informed me. "All we have to do is go to the back of the track where the barns are, and there is always a break in the fence somewhere. We will go either under it or over it, but we will get in."

"I've been to Randall Park many times with my father. He has something to do with racetracks." At that time, I did not know what a bookmaker was, but that was his father's vocation. Nick would follow his way of making a living when he got to the age of majority. Lo and behold, there were gates in the fence on the backside and one of the stable boys saw us trying to sneak in to the track. He went to the gate and surreptitiously allowed us to enter. Well, hallelujah, there we were in amongst the racehorses and the people that were intimately involved in the operation of this enterprise: the stable boys, hot walkers, exercise boys, trainers, owners, and hanger-on's.

Of course, my interest was these beautiful animals and I must admit I had a little fear, because, as I went from one stall to the next, each horse had its own personality. Some stuck their nose out to be petted; others tried to nip you. I learned pretty quickly when the ears were flattened, it was a warning he might not be accepting of your charms. Others acted as if they couldn't care less. However, I suspected the ones that showed an interest thought there might be a treat in my hand.

We became friendly with some of the grooms and jockeys that were there. They asked us what we were doing. We truthfully said we loved horses and had hitchhiked from Youngstown to see them. Well, you never would have believed the concern that came over them.

"There is no way we'll let you hitchhike back," one of the jockeys said,

One of the other guys said he knew a friend who lived in Youngstown and would see that we got home before our parents missed us and that is exactly what happened. They insisted on getting us back right then, and so, this little adventure ended. I will never forget the brotherhood and camaraderie that those folks had for one another. The hustle, the bustle, the smells and the people made a deep impression on me and those impressions lasted a lifetime. By the way, our parents never did find out.

John "Jack" Bradley

While playing golf, I fortuitously met a gentleman named John Jack Bradley, a person that spent his entire life as a jockey, trainer, and owner of racehorses. Jack, starting at about ten years old, with blond hair, blue eyes, and a rather slight build, and a strong love of racehorses, started hot walking thoroughbred horses and eventually became an exercise boy, the youngest at the track. School, at this point in his life was history, as he probably left after finishing the fifth grade, much to the consternation of his parents, who had earlier come to the realization that his home was at the track and where his future was going to be. It was not unusual in that long ago age to quit school and start working at a tender age, most likely on the family's farm.

Jack had no concern for injuries, and there were many. Remember, as an exercise boy, you rode any horse that an owner, or trainer, wanted to work that day. In my experience with thoroughbred horses, they tend to be high strung. They were never meant to be pleasure-riding mounts. Nothing fancy, they knew how to run and run fast; that is what they did and is what they were expected to do.

Many of the young colts were barely familiar with a saddle, yet here was a young boy of ten on top of a twelve-hundred-pound volcano, never knowing when that colt, or filly, would erupt. Jack rode his first race as a full-fledged jockey at the age of fifteen, even though he was required to be sixteen, Jack was able to hide his true age.

Winners and Losers

The first race he ran was in a maiden race, where neither the horses nor the jockeys had ever won a race. He talked the owner into putting him on one of his horses because he still had some remuneration coming.

"Instead of paying me, put me up on something," he said and this owner put him up on something, a horse that was really a jumper.

This mount had never raced and would never race again. The owner knew this horse had no chance and the tote board confirmed his suspicions, a ninety-nine to one shot. The trainer only wanted a workout for the horse just out of curiosity, to see if the colt had any speed at all. Can you imagine what a hero Jack would have been, if he could have kicked that animal in the ass and finished first? Well, Jack was fired up and believed that he could win with this horse.

Youth should be served. The perfect ending would be, after breaking from the gate Jack would have a clear view of the entire race, because the entire field was in front of him, but not for long. Jack would take the colt to the inside, on the rail, riding a brilliant race, weaving in and out, between horses, and in the stretch, he would take him to the rail with a perfectly executed hand ride. Blazing past the wire, where he would stand up in the stirrups, bring his whip above his head and glowed in the adulation of the crowd. Immortality awaited.

Alas, that was not to be. *Jack finished last!* Crestfallen, he had to wait for his next ride and wait he did. After a rather long interval, he had another chance. He was sure, this time, he would do better. His expectations quite a bit blunted this time around, he gave it his mighty best, but he finished, you guessed it, last again!

Feeling terribly discouraged. Jack refused to let himself stay down. One night, he and his brother went out for a snack and ice cream. His brother was looking over the racing form.

"Jack do you know you are riding for Hirsch Jacobs tomorrow?" his brother blurted out.

Jacobs was one of the noted trainers in racing at the time.

"Get the hell out of here, why do you want to poke it at me, at a time like this," Jack said.

"Jack, Jack, it's absolutely true. If you don't believe me, here, look at the form."

There it was in print. Jack was going to ride for one of the best trainers at the track. That meant the horse wasn't some broken down, has-been that had seen better days. Jack could not believe it. Here he was a bug jockey—bug meaning a new jockey that had little experience—and had finished last in his previous two races. Why in the hell would Jacobs want him to ride for the Jacobs Stable?

Jack had a difficult time sleeping that night. The next day he showed up early in the paddock where they saddle the horses before the race. Jacobs was already there. Jack barely knew the man. They only had a nodding acquaintance prior to that.

Hirsch Jacobs

In a quavering rather thin voice, Jack asked Mister Jacobs why he had selected him for this particular ride. Jacobs being taller than Jack, drew himself up and looked down at him,

"I'm going to be straight with you son. As you know, I have a host of jockeys under contract, but as of yesterday, I've had two of my boys down with the flu and one injured working a new colt. I looked all over the track for replacements, but none were available. I've seen the two races you were in, and though you finished last in both races, I recognized you had done the best you could with what you had. I'd seen you working horses every morning and I liked the way you carried yourself. You rode carefully, not wanting to injure your mount. Now, the colt you will be up on, Flying Fort, we have high hopes for. So, your instructions for today are, give him a nice outing, stay the hell out of trouble, and bring him back in one piece. If he shows even a small hitch in his stride when the race is over, I will personally shoot you."

At the appointed time, Jack bolted onto the saddle, and with those instructions ringing in his ears, he made his way to the track, where he would start the warm-up session. It did not take long to realize he was up on a fractious colt, the colt too full of himself, or with a case of the nerves, or there was something not quite right with him. Jack had a real worry that he would not be able to bring him into the starting gate. If the horse became too agitated, they would not be able to load, and the horse would be scratched from the race. If that happened, Jack would hope that Jacobs would shoot him and be quick about it, because the embarrassment would have been too much. If Jacobs did not kill him, he would do it himself.

Broke Maiden

Well, the colt went in all right, and soon, the bell went off and an enormous explosion took place under Jack. He found himself on the rail in the pack about third or fourth place. Most jockeys would pay to be there, but not Jack. With the instructions still in his head, he was not about to get this colt injured running in the pack, possibly getting kicked by another runner, or, worse yet, if a spill occurred that could end this colt's career forever. With that thought in mind, he maneuvered him to the outside and took him wide, where he had to run much faster than the field. Jack knew that this probably cost him the race, but, by God, he was going to get this horse back in one piece as Jacobs had instructed him to do. As the race continued, Jack's horse, to his amazement, gained ground on the leaders. On that glorious day, Jack broke his maiden and finished, you guessed it, *FIRST*!

George Woolf and Seabiscuit

What follows is one of the low points in Jacks memory. Still in his first year as a fledgling jockey, he was racing at Santa Anita. A celebrated jockey by the name of George Woolf was in the race that day. As Jack remembered him, he was a rather laconic young man, never speaking much and he kept to himself. He was the jockey who rode Seabiscuit in the famous match race with War Admiral, a race that was the highlight of the movie, *Seabiscuit.* He was very much focused on his personal problems and trying to keep himself in racing. Like most jockeys, Woolf had a weight problem that threatened to torch his career. On top of that, he was diabetic, but, more than that, to compound his problems, he drank in order to take the edge off his appetite. All of this unhealthy lifestyle came home to roost in this particular race. Riding a horse called Please Me, he passed out and fell headfirst onto the track! He was taken to the hospital immediately, but passed away the next morning.

This made a large impression on Jack, who knew the pressure of trying to keep the money flowing in, regardless of the consequences. Even though he was not married at the time, he could sympathize with the jockeys who had obligations and would do anything to keep their weight down. This included steam rooms, eating very little, purging what they did eat and more than that, not being opposed to taking weight reducing drugs. Along with this they continued running and exercising as much as their little bodies could stand and finally, getting aboard young thoroughbreds that were going to give you all you could handle three or four times a day.

Jack did attend the funeral for George Woolf and one of the most poignant moments at the wake involved Gene Autry, who rose and sang a very stirring song called "Empty Saddles in The Old Corral." This put a resolve in Jack's mind. At a time when he would start having weight problems, which would require extreme solutions, he would quit racing and try training horses. Eventually, that is what happened, but not before one more incident I want to relate. This happened with a great jockey named Eddie Arcaro.

In a high stakes race, that had many of the leading jockeys of the day entered, one was Eddie Arcaro, a renowned Hall of Fame jockey. Jack had an excellent race and managed to finish second to Eddie. Apparently Arcaro, who was known for his aggressiveness, and because of a thirst to be the best jockey ever, as was his style, interfered with a couple of horses in the stretch, as he made a rush for the wire on a horse that was tiring and probably lugged to the rail. The two horses that finished third and fourth lodged a protest and it was upheld by the track stewards. Arcaro was disqualified and Jack was declared the winner.

Well, Eddie was in a titanic rage and thought Jack was the jockey that made the protest. He confronted Jack in the jockey's room and spit a veritable torrent of venom at Jack, who, of course had no part in the events as Arcaro thought they had happened. Before Jack could respond, Eddie reached up and slapped him, much as you would a child. This sent Jack's anger up a few notches, and even though he was younger than Arcaro, but he was larger, and hit Eddie with a blow to the face, sending Eddie down. He struggled to his feet, but before he got his wits about him, Jack hit him again, and again, he went down. This time, when he regained his composure, all the fight had gone out of him and he turned and walked away. As happens in many cases like this, Arcaro eventually became a good friend.

There are so many things that could be said about Mr. Jack Bradley, such as the accolades that have been accorded him at various racetracks and also the near and great celebrities that he worked with. Some made him glad, and some made him mad.

I think the highlight of Jack's life was the wonderful love he had for his wife, Sue, married 56 years, not only his lover, but his partner, mother confessor, fellow traveler, and the glue that held the family together during some very trying times.

Eventually, Jack entered the twilight of his life, his wife had passed on, and he resided in an assisted care facility. As with him, many of us, after having tasted life's sweet pleasures, will eventually have to face the infirmities of old age and the eventuality of the *forever sleep.*

And yet he had one more hurrah. Churchill Downs the bastion and cradle of horseracing in America, knowing that Jack Bradley was nearing the final chapter of life, named a race in honor of Jack for all the things he had done for horseracing. On the appointed day, his children picked him up and drove him to the track. They wanted to surprise him and did not tell him of the honor and recognition he was to receive. But Jack knew something was afoot, so it was not a complete surprise when he was asked to come to the winners circle after the race that was named the "Jack Bradley Memorial Race."

Standing there with a few friends listening to the short speech and the ceremony with photographers flashing pictures, his thoughts returned to days of yore. He thought of his wife, Sue, and all the friends that should have been standing with him. In his mind's eye he looked around and they were with him once again.

Jack Bradley passed away a few weeks after this last hurrah. As with him, if we are lucky to have lived long enough, all of us, after having undergone, the animation and vivacity life holds, the good times, and the bad times. Yes, we will eventually have to face the infirmities of old age and timeless eternity.

Remember birth is a natural occurrence, so is death.

This brought to mind an inscription on a gravestone I read that seems appropriate.

Pause stranger as you pass by,
As you are now, So once was I,
As I am now, So you will be
Prepare to follow me.

Daily Racing Form
Sunday July 21st 2013

Winners and Losers

John M. "Jack" Bradley, a longtime trainer on the New York Thoroughbred circuit and a former jockey, died Sunday in an assisted-living home in Loudon County, Tenn., of thyroid cancer, according to his daughter. Bradley was 83.

After serving in the U.S. Marine Corps, Bradley turned to training and served as an assistant for several years before striking out on his own. In addition to New York, Bradley trained in Florida, Maryland, Louisiana, and Illinois.

Steve Juliano

I present my third and last person in this chapter, Steve Juliano, a little fellow who is truly a Damon Runyon character. Being Italian, hailing from the sidewalks of New York and enjoying much of the delightful cuisine of southern Italy, gave him a rather enlarged girth, a short stature and slightly balding, accorded him a look of impetuosity with a pleasing countenance. He was loquacious and a rather entertaining gentleman to be around. He had a fondness for wagering on sporting events, but, more than that, he was an entrepreneur.

Ron Chicone

After graduating high school, he held a few different jobs, eventually leading him into a bowling pro shop. Okay, now tell me, how many people do you know owned a bowling pro shop? This was a first for me.

Personally, I had a misspent youth, and as I recall, the bowling alleys that I frequented always had a poolroom connected to them. Now, this is only my perception of bowling alleys. I'm sure, nowadays, they call them entertainment centers or family centers or some such thing. The interesting thing about those particular enterprises was the fascinating characters that hung out there, a coterie of guys who fancied themselves investment gurus, or in my vernacular, sharks and hustlers.

It was always my discovery that these benefactors of mankind all had a fast way to make money. Work was never involved, and consequently, not one of them had much in the way of personal affluence. Steve was of a different persuasion, he did not mind toiling for his daily bread, which led him into the most natural thing in the world for an Italian to own, a pizzeria, or, in the parlance of the day, a pizza parlor. Steve did well enough as a capitalist, owning a venture that was a natural for him.

If I may be somewhat of a psychoanalyst, Steve had, even to this day, a problem with low self-esteem. I'm sure this stemmed from his childhood and growing up in a family that would inadvertently use phrases to put you down, they did not realize how much it hurt young, impressionable boys or girls.

One of the favorite words that Italian families use is *stupido* or *stupidone*, so any time you did something that may not have been in the accepted manner, you were dumb, a *stupidone*. I know that word well because I am Italian, and my grandfather thought that was my name. Whenever my friends or I would gather, his favorite utterance was, "Here comes that bum-a-gang." Now don't get me wrong; I did love my Pappy. That was just the way he expressed his admiration for, let us say, an under-achieving young man.

I cannot go on without giving one example of my grandfather's broken English. Coming from a steel mill town there used to be a company with the name Sheet and Tube Steel Company, my grandfather's vernacular; "the shit-in-a-tube still company."

Well, back to Steve; actually Steve had, and still does have, an excellent intellect, but the lure of the racetrack was very strong and he found himself at the New York tracks most days. Of course, this led to betting, which led to losing money, which led to the mistaken belief that he could beat the ponies, and *this* led to a search for a betting system that would beat the track odds. Every bettor has heard of the one guy who made a living betting the ponies, so he naturally assumed there's no reason that he couldn't do the same thing, an erroneous assumption, to be sure. If you can find the man who beats the track, please introduce him to me, because if he has a system that wins, allow me in on it, and it shouldn't be long before we will own the world.

Gamblers for the most part die broke. As an example, let me relate this little tale of woe. There used to be a guy they called Nick the Greek, Nick Dandolos, a very well-known and famous gambler, He was so good, that he set the gambling odds on sporting events for the Las Vegas casinos. He became well known when from January 1949 to May 1949, Dandolos played a two-person "heads up" poker match against Johnny Moss where the two played virtually every variation of the game that existed at the time. The game, set up by Benny Binion the owner of Binion's Casino in Las Vegas as a tourist attraction, is widely credited as being the inspiration for the modern day World Series of Poker.

At the end of this five-month poker marathon, down an estimated $2–4 million, Dandolos uttered what has become one of the most famous poker quotes ever: "Mr. Moss, I have to let you go." Nick the Greek died broke and owed money to all of his friends.

Steve, being of sound mind and deep intellect, did find another way. "If you can't beat em, join em." Well that makes sense doesn't it? All you have to do is find some money, buy some horses and you're in the toughest business possible to be in. But, just think; you are now an insider and now you are spending time with the jockeys and other owners. Why, *hell*, you even know the track stewards and you are friendly with the handicappers and the clockers. If you can't win then, when could you win?

Steve found another cohort, a guy by the name of Herb Schwartz, who had as much passion for the track as he did, and together they decided to go to the Keeneland Auction sales in Kentucky. They spent $13,000 dollars and came away with two horses, a colt called Steal A Dance, and a filly called Cute N Crafty. The colt, they eventually had to geld to make him calmer, but he did well on the track. Paying handsome dividends in winnings before he became too old to race, they retired him. All in all, they did well enough with their investment in the colt.

Cute N Crafty was another story. She had produced two winners in her only two foals. Her pedigree was similar to a horse called Affirmed, a Triple Crown winner. Steve and Herb knew they had a mare that could possibly bring in a mighty big penny at the Keeneland sales. They thought long and hard about this decision to put her in the auction, but finally the pressing matter of money made the decision for them. So they brought Cute N Crafty to Keeneland in Kentucky and entered her in the sale.

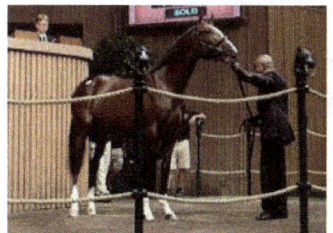 

Keeneland Auction Sales

As they entered the large arena, their nerves were on edge. The reserve they had placed on this mare was $60,000, the minimum price they would accept and had no idea whether the bidding would go that high. If it did not, that meant driving back to New York with empty pockets, the trip having been for naught and their hopes dashed, along with their ability to continue dining in a healthful manner.

As they watched the other horses being sold before Cute N Crafty came to the sales ring, the prices seemed to be going well. This only served to heighten their anticipation, and of course, time seemed to be dragging along by contrast. Finally after an eternity, Cute N Crafty was presented and the call of the auctioneer filled the arena. The bidding started out slowly with the first bid being $10,000 and the bidding continued in increments of one or two thousand dollars. When it reached $50,000 there was a long pause in the bidding. The hearts of our two entrepreneurs were sinking to the well-worn floor, where many others once resided. Suddenly, an increment of $10,000 was presented that brought the bidding to $60,000, a great relief to both men. Steve turned and stretched to see who had made the bid. It was Laz Barrera, a noted trainer at that time. Of course, if Barrera was interested, he was probably bidding for the Wolfsons, who were the owners of Affirmed. They knew the price would go much higher, and higher it did. When it reached $100,000 Steve slid so far down in his seat that his ample rear end was almost on the floor. He couldn't believe what he was hearing. Not in his wildest dreams did he think this mare would bring this much. The biding continued until the hammer came down at $130,000. Steve's knees were so weak by this time that he could not jump up and down for joy. The party got under way that night and continued all the way back to New York.

The next morning, back at Belmont Racetrack, the happy racehorse entrepreneurs went to a restaurant called Liz's Kitchen. It's located on the backstretch and caters to all of the racetrack personnel, jockeys, agents, trainers, etc., but not limited to them. The famous and not-so-famous could be found there. The party continued with much backslapping and copious amounts of coffee, combined with other added ingredients to increase the proof of the coffee, were hoisted as a salute to the two enterprising gentlemen.

Liz was a black lady who didn't take any crap from anyone, but a very hilarious lady nonetheless. One day, Jack Klugman came in, a star of the TV series *The Odd Couple*. Being Jewish, he asked Liz for bagels and lox. Liz looked at him for a long moment and finally said, "Look around this place; does it look like we sell bagels and lox here? But I'll tell you what, when is the next time you are planning on coming in?"

"I'll probably be back next week," he said.

"Well, next week, for you, I will get bagels and lox."

During the week, she asked everybody about bagels and lox and where she could buy the very best. She acquired the best she could find, at no small effort on her part, and had them ready for Mr. Klugman when he returned.

The next week, when Krugman's friend returned without Klugman, Liz said, "Hey, where's that Jew boy you had in here last week?"

His friend explained that Jack could not make it that week and Liz exploded. She kept a little whip in back of the counter, in case a customer (all customers were really her friends) got out of hand and she'd whack him with the whip. This was done all in fun, of course.

"When you see that Jew boy, tell him I'm going to give him a whipping that he'll never forget," she said with a wink of her eye.

Meanwhile, Steve was basking in the congratulations of his friends, and if I know Steve, he picked up tabs for all of his friends. Thus, the party continued.

It was not long after that Steve and his partner broke up, but it was amicable. I believe Steve now felt he had enough capital to expand his own stable. By this time, Florida bestowed upon him his training license, providing another source of income and adding more horses from other owners.

Together with his own string, the travel back and forth to the various tracks in New York, New Jersey and Florida put an additional strain on Steve. All of this took its toll, not only in money, but late nights with sick horses and early mornings up before dawn, being at the track at 5:30 a.m. to train and work out his menagerie. Even though he was able to struggle along, the handwriting was on the wall.

The legacy from Cute N Crafty was dissipating and Steve, being the consummate capitalist, began searching his fertile imagination for another source of income. Soon, a light went on. How about a limousine service exclusively for the people at the track who had to come and go, like jockeys, trainers, and owners? Other limousine drivers did not know the barns and backstretch like Steve, who could take you immediately to the barn that the client requested.

Steve's service prospered until he owned four limos, however, fate intervened, and the tax law changed and his clients were no longer able to deduct the cost of the limo ride from their taxes. *Oops,* there went the limo business.

Steve's parents passed away and he became the sole keeper of his brother, who was, unfortunately, born with Down's Syndrome. Steve had a boundless love for his brother and it was incumbent on him to care for him properly, which meant settling down in one place. Steve chose Florida. He bought a small condominium and commenced giving his brother a good life, knowing that a person with Down's Syndrome had a limited time to spend on this earth. Steve, now being up in years, did not have the wherewithal for a secure retirement, but with the resources he had, he provided for his brother, Bernard, until his brother passed away.

When I look back on Steve's life, I feel he reached the pinnacle of his chosen profession and the enjoyment that he took from it was immense. His life was filled with— for lack of a better word—*LIFE.* Could he have chosen a better career path? Of course, but then what would he have had? A little more money perhaps, but no memories, no excitement, no thrills, no really great friends. The problem with achieving a long life, other than the infirmities that are a natural consequence of an extended life, is that *friends gradually disappear.*

What I have tried to do in the foregoing is to give you a sense of what life at the races is all about. You can experience every emotion that exists: love, hate, laughter, riches, poverty, loyalty, many friends, and extreme emotional connections with people and animals.

What comes to mind when I think about horseracing? If you love a ride on a really severe roller coaster, then you will love being a part of that grand institution.

Originator of General Motors
William Crapo Durant

The man the world forgot, the giant who almost single-handedly brought our country and the world into the Automobile Age, the Architect of wondrous things that are a part of our everyday life, my admiration is unrestrained for the authors who have gone before me in the iteration of this man's life. I have nothing but the most profound veneration for their understanding of William "Billy" Durant.

My intention in writing this chapter is to eulogize this truly special, one-of-a kind, extraordinary man who gave so much and asked so little. Generous, without pretensions, devoid of many of the character flaws that are inflicted upon so many of that generation, this utter disregard of pretensions is the overriding factor in following the theme of this book, *Winners and Losers*.

I will not follow the minutia of the other missives that have been written about Billy, but one book of distinction is: *Billy Durant Creator of General Motors* by Lawrence R. Gustin, a beautifully written work, with an immense amount of research and background instituted into this manuscript.

In this Chapter, I will relate only those accomplishments that directly affected the world we live in. For me, it would be hard to fathom a world without names like, Chevrolet, Buick, Oldsmobile, Pontiac, Cadillac, and Frigidaire, with slogans that bring on a bit of nostalgia, like "baseball, hotdogs, apple pie and Chevrolet, or, "When better cars are made, Buick will make them." Describing Mr. Durant is damn near impossible, without making him a godlike figure, but in his personal life, he was very human.

In our own experiences, I believe that most people would have the ability to describe a person who was driven with an ambition beyond ordinary comprehension. Generally, these people are without scruples or personal loyalties, and will ignore their home life to the extent that many divorces are a result of this inattention. They have a fire within their bellies that cannot be quenched. Many of this ilk go on to great success, but others that have failed arrive at a time in their lives when they are older and they look around to see only the wreckage of their lives.

Some of this is true in describing Billy. Guilty of the utter inattention to his home life in his first marriage, he had a wonderfully successful second marriage, to a much younger woman than he, a beauty who fit his lifestyle. Long absences from home were a part of his life, and she got along well with that situation, realizing, that was part and parcel of the avocation that he chose. His scruples were beyond question. Investors who invested with Billy in his many ventures could be assured of success, or he would refund the entire amount of loss from his own pocket. His positive attributes were many; silver tongued, soft spoken, exuding confidence and commanding respect, truly a visionary, who had an enthusiastic manner that contributed to his outstanding salesmanship. Short, but rather handsome in a benign way. He was about five-six, but belied his short stature with his erectness and posture, paired with' an easy, casual manner. Looking upon his visage gave you a feeling of confidence in his ability to be successful in whatever endeavor he was expounding upon.

∞∂∞

Born in Boston, Massachusetts in 1861, he spent his formative years in New England, and for the rest of his life, he would have a Boston accent, pronouncing his name as *Doo*rant rather than Du*rant*.

Billy relocated with his family to Flint, Michigan at about age ten. Other relations had preceded him, established roots and became well-respected members of the community. In fact, his grandfather, whose name was Henry Crapo, a rather stern and foreboding person, had been Governor of Michigan from 1865 to 1869. Durant's father, who was never liked by the Governor was a well-spoken individual, but with a few debilitating faults, not the least of which was drinking and gambling excessively. He eventually disappeared from Billy's life and was never heard from again, certainly no great loss. Much of Billy's personality was inherited from his dad. His easygoing manner, his touch with the common man and his gambling instincts were all handed down. However, Billy was always a teetotaler, probably the result of seeing his father in a drunken stupor most of the time.

Most gamblers have an utter disregard for money and this was so in Durant's life as well, confirmed by the fact that Billy was broke or near broke several times. His saving grace was his past successes and the confidence that others placed in him. This made it rather easy for him to raise capital when he needed it.

A later edition of the original cart that revolutionized America

An incident that occurred early in his career was particularly fortuitous. As young William was hurrying to a meeting of the local utility company where he was an officer, he stopped and carried on a conversation with Josiah Dort, who was part owner of the hardware store. One of the employees of the hardware store, Johnny Alger, pleasantly asked Durant if he would like a ride to the meeting in his new acquisition, a cart with a new type of suspension system. Billy, who was usually in a hurry, agreed to the offer. As Billy rode to his meeting in this horse cart that looked like it belonged as a sulky in a trotting race, he gradually became aware of how pleasurable that this ride was. It had an absence of the inexorable bumping and swaying side to side that other carts of its day were imbued with. He immediately charged over to the factory where this cart was produced, The Cold Water Road Cart Co., and introduced himself to a little older man that he took to be the owner. The old fellow had little to say and wondered what this audacious individual wanted. Billy, being familiar with craftsmen who had little to say, and preferred to let their hands do the talking, started by asking if he was the owner of that fine establishment that made this well-built cart. Finally, the old fellow introduced himself, not without some trepidation.

"I am Thomas O'Brian. What is the nature of your visit?"

Billy then extolled the virtues of the little cart that O'Brian had put together. Being the businessman that he was, he carefully pointed out the superior characteristics, but at the same time, held his enthusiasm back a little. He then went on to say that he was an experienced salesman and thought he could increase the sales of this vehicle if he could purchase a portion of the business. Thomas looked him in the eye trying to ascertain the seriousness of his offer. After a length of time, having not spoken a word, he turned around, walked into the next room, and eventually returned with another gentleman in tow. He introduced this person as his partner. William H. Schmedlen.

"It is my understanding that you wish to purchase this business," Schmedlen said to Billy,

Billy went on hurriedly to explain he only meant a *portion* of the entity, being that he did not have a lot of funds at this time.

"We're not interested in partners," Schmedlen said. "Too many hands in the soup would spoil the broth. However, if you could produce $1500 dollars, we may be persuaded to sell lock stock and barrel."

Billy was surprised at the small amount of money it would take to acquire this delightful and handsome cart. Not having the $1,500 in hand, his keen mind started working on where these funds might be obtained.

The name Crapo carried an immense amount of weight in the state, and many of his relatives worked in the financial industry. Billy had no intention of asking them for the money, thinking, if he failed in this under taking, it would reflect badly on his entrepreneurial skills and diminish his reputation among the very people that he might approach for funding in the future. This is not to say that Billy did not approach this new exciting opportunity with the complete confidence and enthusiasm he would use to approach every business deal in the future. Durant did not know it at the time, but his future was probably going to be transcendent with this one transaction.

Billy eventually contacted a bank that was willing to loan him the money. A gentleman by the name of Robert J. Whaley was the loan officer and Durant, in later years, would credit this man with the establishment of General Motors and reward him handsomely.

Durant and Josiah Dort

Josiah Dort later approached Billy with an offer to buy into the business and become a fifty/fifty partner and Durant willingly agreed. Of course, the next problem was the selling of this cart. Now, showing his salesmanship ability, he decided to show it at state fairs. At the very first fair, he managed to acquire a blue ribbon as best cart in the fair. The new name of the company was The Flint Road Cart Company, and now, it had a slogan, "The Famous Blue Ribbon Line of Carriages." At that fair, Billy was able to take orders for one-hundred carts, with no idea how he would fill those orders, but that was just the start. After visiting George C. Cribbs & Company, he walked away with an order to supply them with thirty-five carts every ten days.

Clearly, Durant had an immense success on his hands, way before he was able to supply the product. Being the affable sort, with an exceptionally agile mind, quickly decided to bring another manufacturer into the picture. If his factory was not ready to supply this cart, he would find a company that could. Searching out the most quality qualified manufacturer in the business. He settled on a highly respected carriage maker, William Paterson, Flint's largest carriage maker, producing two a day and employing twelve men. Paterson was respected for the quality of the carriages he produced, but he had the scruples of a prowling wolf, as William Durant would discover in time.

Paterson asked Billy for $12.50 per cart, a clearly excessive sum, but Billy thought he could get twice that amount and he knew that it was only a matter of time that all the carts would be produced in his own factory. Little did he know it would be sooner than he expected. Later on, Paterson gave Billy the proverbial screwing by cutting Billy out and producing the carts for himself. Even though, Billy was forced to do business with this unscrupulous person, he never forgot what happened and vowed never to let it occur again. It's lessons learned the hard way that are lessons learned best. Durant would, thereafter, not only produce his own product, but also centralize any peripheral parts he had to job out, by finding a way to make them himself. Later when he was asked the secret of his ability to sell his products, he proclaimed it was not his ability as much as it was the products' ability to sell themselves.

Thus, this amazing $2,000 dollar company was able to produce four-thousand units in its first year of operation and became one of the largest cart manufacturers in the country. It was the precursor to the General Motors organization. Durant, was a millionaire by the time he was forty years old. This budding superman had one feature of his aurora that would make him omnipotent, the ability to recognize latent genius and surround himself with extremely talented individuals. Among the names that he discovered: Dort, Nash, Aldrich, Mott,

Champion, Chevrolet, Hardy, Slocum, Wesson, Webster, et al.

∞∂∞

It was said of Durant that he could walk into a new area, find the best salesmen, hire them away from whatever they were doing, and make them "Durant Men." Durant could sell a salesman a career, a customer a cart, a company a territory. With his over-the-top enthusiasm and optimism, he would be able to infect everyone he added to his team with a dream of riches far beyond anything they had ever thought about. More than that, because of their newfound enthusiasm, they became inventors and innovators par excellence. It was not long before the carriage company would have territories clear across the United States.

In 1895, Billy changed the name of the company to the Durant-Dort Carriage Co and now they started adding other companies that Billy became interested in. One was a bicycle company that failed. Bicycles eventually went the way of the buggy whip when other forms of transportation became popular. We must remember then, as now, when starting a new venture it always behooves you to use other people's money, if at all possible. The investors in this venture, of course, lost their entire investment.

Durant, being of high standards, felt it was a black mark on his business acumen if people lost money in something he had promoted. He went to his partner and told him that he thought the Durant-Dort Company should reimburse them their investment. Dort, of course, would never go against Billy's wishes, but did feel that, when you invested in something, you should understand that there was a risk of loss as well as a potential to make a substantial profit. Billy said, because those investors believed in him, as long as he had the wherewithal to reimburse them they should do it. He felt that it was good public relations as well as good business. He was of the opinion that good will would pay handsome dividends in the future. As usual, he was correct.

About 1900, Durant was faced with another significant

problem. Trusts were trying to control the distribution of carriages and anything connected with the carriage business. This was Billy's province and he became a "trustbuster" in name and in fact. As the trust bought up companies, Durant stepped in and lowered his prices to such a degree that the trusts with high leveraging could not compete and either went bankrupt or sold out for what they could get—pennies on the dollar. In the process of trust busting, Billy had to work so hard, he survived on only four or five hours of sleep a night and everyone around him was required to work almost as hard as he did. However, it literally caused a trusted lieutenant, A. B. Hardy, to come near to collapse. Billy could see this happening and suggested Hardy take his wife on an extended European excursion. This turned out to be an excursion that would change the entire world for him and for Billy.

While in Paris, Hardy attended the Paris Exposition, which was thoroughly enjoyable and piqued his interest in a newfangled gadget that had been around for a few years, but seemed certain to become more popular.

Horseless Carriage

Winners and Losers

At first, Hardy could not see why. They were called horseless carriages and were essentially a cart with a small, one-cylinder motor that was noisy, weak, emitting smokey, stinky fumes that were unpleasant to the senses, but had one saving grace: it could get from point A to point B without the use of a horse. Hardy studied this new thing with growing interest, and finally, excitement set in. His communications to Durant showed his attraction for this faddish device and thought there was a possibility this motor driven vehicle could be improved upon for commercial gain.

Billy, surprisingly, was unimpressed. He was already aware of this new invention and thought of all the drawbacks it had, among them frightening horses. It was one time in his life that his vision was not intact. Of course, it's hard to understand why his zeal was less than what one would expect from a visionary, but there were compelling reasons that Billy had that clouded vision. We must realize that he was the grand master in the U. S. A. of carriages. If this new fad caught on, it certainly would threaten the cornerstone of his wealth.

Flint Wagon Works

Hardy returned from the continent in 1901 and immediately went to the Flint Wagon Works and proclaimed to one and all that the days of the carriage were numbered. Hardy himself had an urge to get in to the automotive business and it was not long after that he scratched that itch, much to his regret. He organized The Flint Automobile Co. and started producing a fine roadster that had much leather and polished brass. He put together about fifty-two roadsters when he ran into another serious problem. The Association of Licensed Automobile Manufacturers, a group of automobile producers licensed under the 1895 patent of George B. Selden, used this patent to collect royalties from automobile manufacturers. The royalties owed to them by Hardy was $50 per car. Taking it to court, Hardy had fifty-two actions against him. He angrily went out of business and left Flint. He went to Iowa, where he became general manager of a carriage company, and remained until he was called back to Flint by Billy Durant, his former employer. Henry Ford finally challenged this Association of Manufacture's in court, and after many years of litigation, he was able to break their hold on the business.

At the same time, in 1901, Durant was growing bored with the carriage business, which was going along nicely and did not need his attention. He found a rather new interest: the stock market. This appealed to Billy's natural instincts. Gambling and action was what he craved, and not only that, the market was in its ascendancy and quite a bit of money was being made there. Being the optimistic sort, Billy scored large gains that seemed to him to be manna from heaven, but it was only because of his expertise in business, and his ability to size up a company that he felt able to divine its future, or so he thought. When a market break came along, he always thought it would eventually return to its winning ways, and in those days, he was right. However, when the 1930s came along the market continued down year after dreary year and 1929, before the crash, would be the zenith of Billy's meteoric career.

Unhappily married, Durant stayed away from home as much as he could and the stock market was his excuse to stay in New York, where Wall Street was located, and return home

Winners and Losers

infrequently. His wife, Clara, and their two children, Margery and Russell, were left behind in Flint. Because Billy had an inherent regard for principles that had guided his life, he spent much of his time while away from home in a deep funk, since his belief system was one that would not allow him to spend time with other women.

During this period of his life, he had tried to resign from the board of his own company, but the other directors would not hear of it. This move by the other officers would lead to his eventual return to Flint and a progression into the flourishing automobile business.

Buick

In 1903, the Buick Motor Car Company was little more than a research firm that had great ideas and superior improvements in engine design, with not a farthing to implement their splendid engineering ideas.

This firm was headed up by David Dunbar Buick, the person who had patented the adhesion of porcelain to cast iron that made the advent of the modern bathtub and other bathroom and plumping fixtures possible. Now, he had much needed partners, because of his constant need for capital. He took in Ben and Frank Briscoe, brothers who had some success in other businesses, thinking they had the resources to fund a small start-up company. The brothers did have some amount of capital, but, after realizing Buick's interests were more in the design and invention field, they figured out that they were positioned to lose what they had. Looking to the future, their crystal ball was showing nothing but losses. Now, they were in the market to find someone to bail them out.

James H. Whiting's interest in automobiles was triggered by Hardy. Mr. Whiting was a man of means, older and more conservative than most others in autos, but an excellent businessman. He could see the great future this new invention had, when he visited Hardy's shop and other manufacturers in his locality. Around the country, there were literally hundreds of startup manufacturers and a great groundswell of automobile aficionados occurring all over the world.

Word got around that Mr. Whiting might be interested in investing in something that interested him, and the brothers Briscoe decided to pay him a visit. The Briscoe's were anxious to have returned the money that Buick had borrowed from them, seeming unduly worried about, the $3900 that Buick owed them.

Whiting, who owned Flint Wagon Works, made an investment of $10,000 and bought Buick, lock stock and barrel, including the famous valve-in-head engine that revolutionized the industry, being more powerful and utilizing fuel more efficiently. In the beginning, the company just concentrated on engines, but eventually produced their first production Buick with a two-cylinder engine.

The company eventually ran into trouble. One problem was with inefficient production concerning their farm division, the other, when they ran into the Selden Interests, which held the patent on automobiles until they were challenged in court by Henry Ford.

The Buick Company was deep in debt and had run through their original capitalization of $37,500. Whiting was now searching for an angel, somebody with deep pockets. As fortune would have it, on a boring train trip out of town, he sat with Fred Aldrich, secretary of the Durant-Dort Carriage Company.

Winners and Losers

Whiting related his problems to Aldrich, as businessmen in related fields are wont to do, especially where it concerned the Selden Interests, a universally hated company and Aldrich, upon hearing of these problems, immediately thought of his sponsor, Durant. He knew that Billy was not as yet caught up in the automobile craze, but, knowing Billy loved a challenge and a good fight, he did not see how Durant could avoid this opportunity.

Billy heard about this situation soon enough. One of the things that moved his thinking in the right direction was the problem of Flint, Michigan losing its standing as the number one vehicle city in the country. However, the primary thing was really his ability to take this company and make it a successful operation. Durant was not naïve. He could easily see, during his time in New York, and entertaining his fascination with the stock market, that automobiles were the future.

In some haste, he went back to Flint and investigated this Buick Company. He did this by talking to the directors and stockholders and taking demonstration drives in the latest Buick automobile. Billy was immensely impressed and decided, at this point, that he would bring this company under his wing. After taking control, Billy found there were creditors that were making large claims for engines that were never delivered. Billy approached the claimants and informed them that if they won, the company would declare bankruptcy and they would receive nothing, or they could go along with the company's restructuring, and as its fortunes improved, they would receive either the engines, or the indebtedness that was owed them. The creditors decided that the line of least resistance would be to go along with Durant, which happened because of Durant's reputation for fair play.

It was time for Billy to get to work. An auto show opened in New York that the silver-tongued maestro attended, and in short order, he came back with over 1,000 orders.

Not everyone was happy with Durant's success. Dort,

Billy's partner in the carriage business, could not understand why Billy lost interest in carriages, when they were having the best year ever. When they talked to Billy about this, he would become so animated talking about automobiles that both Nash and Dort, officers in the Durant-Dort Carriage business, thought he was becoming delusional. The carriage business was liquidated by 1917.

∞∂∞

Billy and Catherine   **1907 Buick**

1907 was a defining year, for Billy. He met a very young girl, 25 years his junior, Catherine Lederer, a friend of his children. They started dating, despite the objections from the girl's mother, but, in view of Durant's prominence, I do not believe the protest was very strongly expressed. Her objections were not based on the fact that he was so much older, but solely on the fact that he was still married. Durant rectified that in 1908, not that long after his new romance started.

An interesting highlight of the divorce proceedings was the fact that a lifelong friend; Dr. Edwin R. Campbell, testified for Clara, to the fact that Billy had ignored his wife for ten years, failed to write to her when she was seriously ill, and repeatedly stated he would not live with her. It becomes enlightening to learn that Billy and the good doctor were good friends indeed, and as a matter of fact, in the year of the divorce, he married

Winners and Losers

Billy's daughter and became associated with Durant's business. I do believe that Billy made sure the divorce was granted and married Catherine the next day. The divorce settlement, $150,000 cash plus securities and was later bolstered by an out-of-court settlement of $2,000,000. Clara then remarried and moved to California.

I think it is important at this point to show why Billy with his high degree of optimism was super successful, and how that same optimism eventually paved the way to complete and utter failure.

In 1907, the Buick factory produced over four-thousand vehicles, even though the country was undergoing a recession and certainly not buying most anything, let alone autos. Billy insisted that his production lines keep going to capacity. He deftly fended off creditors and filled every warehouse he could find with Buicks. One reason for such confidence was that he knew Buick had the best engine available at the time. The second reason was that he knew the downturn was only temporary, as was usually the case. Again, he was right, and when the economy improved, Durant was the only automobile manufacturing company able to supply the enormous public demand. So far, his incredible instincts were intact.

David Dunbar Buick

David Dunbar Buick was another matter; His personality was such that he had a difficult time getting along with other officers in the company. He finally resigned and he was given a generous stipend to live on. Of course, he pissed it away and died a pauper. Does this make you sad? It does me, a brilliant engineer with his common sense impaired.

Frank Briscoe, no stranger to the art of the deal, approached Durant with the idea of consolidating the large automobile companies of which there were many, including Ford, Oldsmobile, Buick, Packard, Peerless, Pierce-Arrow, and others. This was not a new idea to Billy. While in New York, he kicked it around with several colleagues. It was decided at that time that the personalities involved in this business were too individualistic to be organized into a cohesive group. He explained this to Briscoe, pointing out that if you were to include Ford, he would never accept anything but a leadership role. So, all in all, Billy did not believe it would work. However, this did not preclude the idea from his mind. He told Briscoe to talk to a couple of the more important companies and feel them out.

Briscoe felt that he was on to a magnificent idea and could not wait to get started. Straight-away, he went to Ransom E. Olds, who was now heading a company called REO that he had started after he left the Oldsmobile Company in 1904, and named using his three initials. Olds was truly a pioneer at the start of the horseless carriage era, when the automobile was just a gleam in the eye of those in the know. In the year 1897, he was already running about in steam driven horseless carriages. Olds was definitely interested in Briscoe's merger idea.

Next on the agenda, and the key in this whole scheme, would be Henry Ford. He was as big as Buick at this point in time as far as the number of autos produced. Olds and Briscoe approached Ford with a great deal of apprehension, being familiar with the abrasiveness that the young Ford could exhibit at times. He was very outspoken and one who would not mince

Winners and Losers

words when telling you what he thought. Briscoe was pleasantly surprised when he found Ford receptive to the idea.

Briscoe returned to Flint and reported to Durant the seemingly glad tidings. A meeting was hastily arranged, to be held in a hotel room, but was eventually held in Billy's suite at the Pontchartrain Hotel, somewhat furtively to escape any unwanted publicity. Because there was not a cogent plan in existence, the principals, who had been accompanied by officers and financial advisors of their respective companies, started to throw around various proposals. Ford, who everyone realized would be a catalyst, was rather quiet. All of this had to be presented to J. P. Morgan & Company, who would supply the initial funding for the consolidation of the various manufacturers. After spending the entire afternoon discussing the proposals, there was general agreement to return to their homes and do some hard thinking on what had been discussed. They left the meeting with no concrete plans, but at least there seemed to be a general agreement that everyone would have an open mind.

Meetings with J.P. Morgan's attorneys were held in New York. These meetings continued into the summer of 1908. One of the surprises that came from this get-together was that Ford was not interested in consolidation, but in a complete buy out of his company. Durant and others were interested, but the price was too steep. Ford was dropped from these discussions as was a reluctant R. E. Olds. The meetings went on until an agreement between Buick and a Maxwell-Briscoe combine was tentatively formed. The Oldsmobile Company was having problems and their sales were declining. This caught Durant's attention. He contacted the principals involved, a Mr. S. L. Smith, and his sons and received an indication of interest.

In the process of bringing General Motors to fruition, there were interminable meetings; every meeting involving lawyers. As an aside to attorneys that may be reading this, I know from experience that they are deal killers. This comes about because of their strong desire to protect their clients. In many cases, they have a difficult time seeing beyond the contractual terms to the many good things that can come about over time. What primarily killed this proposal was Billy's insistence that he and only he control the money. This went against the Morgan interests, who were very shrewd and usually held the upper hand in any deal. Durant decided to incorporate even though there was only one company.

There were a couple of names proposed for the budding conglomerate, first United Motors that was eventually dropped for International Motor Car Company, the name spelled out in the papers for the original failed consolidation that fell through and owned jointly by Billy and a Mr. Perkins. Billy felt it would not be a problem getting Perkins to relinquish his part ownership of the name, but Billy was wrong. Perkins respectfully declined. Finally, the name General Motors was picked from a list that Billy had provided. Thus, we have the birth of the company that would be a dominant force in the automotive industry, both nationally and internationally.

The Birthday of General Motors Corporation September 16, 1908

After closing on the papers of incorporation, Billy wasted no time leaving New York and heading on his way to Lansing, Michigan. He closed on Buick, paying three million, seven hundred and fifty thousand dollars to make it a part of GM, and then rapidly wrapped up the Oldsmobile situation for $3 million. The financing was handled for the most part by the issuance of stock in the newly formed company. When asked, after going over the Oldsmobile books, whether he had found anything worthwhile in them, he replied with a resounding "No!" When asked if he thought he overpaid for the company, Billy again said no, that the name Oldsmobile was such a venerated name that it was well worth the price. The song, *In My Merry Oldsmobile*, was still popular. If you ever see and hear a barbershop quartet, you will find the song is still part of their repertoire, and I hope it always will be.

Durant saw to it that he acquired a car designed to be worthy of the name. He came up with the Model 10, a small car with a powerful, 4-cylinder, valve-in-head engine. Priced at the lower end, this auto outperformed all other cars in its class, became a best seller, and immediately made Oldsmobile profitable.

While Billy was getting GM going, he would randomly visit various sales showrooms. On one of these visits, a young man by the name of Albert Champion approached him, and offered to sell magnetos or sparkplugs to Durant. After hearing him out, he asked if he thought he could make a sparkplug especially for Buick. Billy was having trouble getting the high performance plugs needed for the car's powerful engine that they had developed. He said he could and Durant offered to buy out his company and put him in his own factory. If successful, a portion of the company would be his. Mr. Champion returned to the stockholders with the offer Durant had proposed. Albert's partners turned this down and became successful in their own right with Champion Sparkplugs, albeit without Mr. Champion. Albert went on to become a champion with GM forming a company called A. C. Sparkplugs. Once again, Billy demonstrated his superior taste in picking relatively unknown-but-talented individuals.

Billy was now on the hunt. He wanted acquisitions, large or small startups. His thinking was, if a large company was putting itself on the block, it meant one of two things; either it was losing money or it was about to lose money. In Billy's mind, that did not in any way negate a possible deal. Billy had this tremendous confidence that he would be able to turn any business around. Small struggling companies were what made Billy's juices start to flow, because that's where the challenges were.

Oakland Motor Car Co. was one such example,. They had a great powerful auto, a unique product, but were having financial problems. Of course, this drew Billy's attention like a hound dog on the scent. Billy sent an emissary to visit with Edward M. Murphy, the company's president and a very progressive, well-organized man. Billy's agent returned with the news that Mr. Murphy was not at this time interested in a merger with GM. Billy never blinked an eye, but made it his goal to become fast friends with Murphy.

It eventually happened, on one faithful day on his way to New York. He stopped by Murphy's place just to say hello, Murphy handed Durant a package. In it, was all of Murphy's stock in Oakland Motors to exchange for GM stock. Billy was so taken aback by this act of generosity that, for a moment, there was a mist in his eyes. Mr. Murphy died soon after this exchange of stock, affording his family a healthy estate, but if he had never made the exchange the company would have been worth virtually nothing after his death. So, for all the businessmen who may be reading this, honey is the lure that attracts the most gifts. Oakland eventually became Pontiac, another phenomenally successful brand.

Henry M. Leland is another name that became important to Bill's future plans. Leland had a reputation as an engineer of quality, from guns to motors, and by 1908, he became head honcho at Detroit Motors, which had morphed into another superlative automobile company named Cadillac. Durant and Leland were direct competitors, and because of their intensity, were not friends.

Ralph Aldrich, brother of Fred Aldrich of the Durant-Dort Carriage Co., stopped in to exchange pleasantries. Billy took this opportunity to ask Ralph if he knew anybody at Cadillac. Billy, like a good attorney, never asked a question that he did not already know the answer. Ralph said he was good friends with Henry Leland; whereupon Billy, displaying a wide smile and a warm personality, asked Ralph to arrange a meeting with Leland. Billy wanted to offer compensation for his services, but felt it would be an affront to a friend and the brother of one of his partners. Therefore, Billy made it clear, if he was successful in this endeavor he would be forever in his debt.

Within two weeks, a meeting was arranged. The meeting would be in Detroit at the Cadillac Hotel. Billy and Leland exchanged pleasantries and immediately got down to business. Durant proposed a buyout totaling $2,500,000. Leland came back with a figure of $3,500,000. Durant told him that he would present the offer to the GM board and see what options they would recommend. Leland immediately shot back that there would be no options, the proposed price was non-negotiable. Billy responded that he would recommend the purchase.

Billy called the board together in New York at the GM offices and gave them the conditions of the purchase and the advantages of the acquisition. A protest from Fred Smith was lodged at this time, reminding Durant that he still owed Smith's father $1,800,000. Billy had truly forgotten about this obligation and notified Leland that, at this time he was unable to complete the purchase of Cadillac, but would respectively request that a meeting in the future be possible, as soon as he was able to satisfy a current obligation.

A few months later, after Billy had fully repaid the loan, he contacted Leland once again and inquired if he was still open to the purchase of his company. Leland said that he was, but on entirely different terms. They arranged to meet at the old Ponchartrain Hotel in Detroit. As the meeting got underway, Leland informed Billy that the price was now $4,750,000, with rather harsh terms. A $500,000 deposit was required as a forfeit amount, with the balance due in 30 days, plus one-percent interest for every three days the payment was late. Billy inquired if they would take any preferred stock and Leland agreed that they would consent to a very tiny part of the purchase price in preferred GM stock. With that out of the way, Billy picked up the phone, called the President of the Peninsular Bank, and told him he had just bought Cadillac. He would require $500,000 immediately to bind the deal and the balance of the purchase price within thirty days. He was prepared to pledge the entire stock of Cadillac and some of GM stock if necessary. He then retained Leland and his son in the management position with a handsome salary and incentives. Durant knew he did not have the time to look for and hire a new team. What better situations, then, to have an experienced team manage the company?

Winners and Losers

In the first two years of GM, Durant bought all of, or an interest in, over twenty different companies. Some were hits, but many more were misses. He felt that his investment in these acquisitions, even though some were failures, was justified for various reasons, not the least of it being patents that he might have use for in the future. But Billy was upsetting many of the people who had a huge interest in one or more of these companies, such as bankers who were holding GM stock as collateral. They were very nervous over the thin limb they felt they were on.

Billy was now on a tangent that often happens to gamblers who are also exhibiting excessive-compulsive behavior. Everyone around him became concerned over the casual way he bought companies and threw away capital. During this period of time, Durant came close to purchasing Ford, but because of the amount of financing that the weight of his companies comprised, the bank turned down his request for an initial $2,000,000. This caused Billy to send a letter to Ford, explaining that he could not arrange financing and would not be able to complete the transaction.

A few years later, Ford was earning 35 million a year. The bankers and others who were instrumental in the collapse of the Ford deal would never forgive themselves, but, truly, they had no other choice. As for Billy, he had no regrets. He felt that he could never have made Ford into the gigantic firm it had become without Henry Ford. Remember that money to Durant was of no concern, only the power that it could afford him.

The trouble for Durant started at the annual bankers meeting in late 1909. The board had been growing more and more rancorous and concerned about the way Billy was throwing money around, along with the way he was running the company. Especially since, only months before, he had tried to buy Ford for $8 million dollars and the bankers killed the deal. They felt General Motors was being run like a one-man serfdom and Billy's organizational abilities were lacking. One of the bankers made a very telling speech, pointing out that the demand for automobile money was so great that it was denying other clients access to enough capital to efficiently operate their respective businesses.

Just to give a perspective on what the bankers group was looking at, Billy had bought the Heany Lamp group of companies after insufficiently scrutinizing their internal documents, he found that their patents, the primary reason why he had bought the outfit in the first place, had been seriously compromised and were now useless. The cost to GM? $12 million dollars. Ouch!

Billy, trying to stem the bad publicity he was receiving, declared a one-hundred-fifty percent dividend. Now, how do you do that with no money? GM had the ability to create additional shares of stock. Yes, that's what it did without increasing the intrinsic value of the stock. Just as inconsequential stock splits do today, the price of GM stock temporarily soared. In 1910, the year started strong, but it was not long before the panic started and Durant, at one point, was going to propose an additional four-hundred percent dividend, which of course never came to fruition. This alone indicated the state of mind that Durant was in—crazy comes to mind.

The stock of GM was steadily losing value and the banks that were holding GM stock were losing collateral value. Just as in football, the coach had to go. The creditors of GM met in August of 1910. At this meeting, they decided there would be a reorganization of GM. At this point, GM was on the verge of collapse. Durant did everything he could to stave off the inevitable. The lights in his office burned to the early morning and he walked the streets in the middle of the night.

This was one time that Billy's powers of persuasion failed. The bankers and creditors got together and formed a plan, a very necessary plan. They were at wits end and realized that, to save them, they would have to extend more capital to GM. Of course this wasn't done in a vacuum. After a perusal of the books and a study of the economic situation in the country, they came to the conclusion it was worth saving the company. Their efforts did not go unrewarded, in that they were to receive about $12 million for their efforts and a 5-year voting trust. If the company then went on to fail, the entire country would have been thrust into a severe depression. Several banks would have been close to bankruptcy, which, in turn, would have caused a run on them. I mention this so that you will understand that the compensation they received was in line with their risk.

Durant was named Vice President and a member of the board, which made him a bitter man. He felt that they stole the company from him, and as the future unfolded, would be run as you would naturally assume a company would be run by a bunch of bankers. The cuts they made were draconian. Every subsidiary and every division across the spectrum was not spared. As Billy watched this explosion occur, it was as if his heart were pulled from his chest and trampled on. After all GM was his baby. Billy looked around and saw nothing remotely resembling the colossus he had built and an implacable resolve formed in him; he would one day be running GM again.

Louis Chevrolet Race Car driver

One of the first people he sought out was a retired race car driver who used to race for Buick with much success by the name of Louis Chevrolet. He very much wanted to build a car to his specifications. Billy, who was not without means and friends, personally set up Louis in a small factory and let him have it. In the meantime, he again approached Flint Wagon Works, which was producing a small car that they were struggling with. The Whiting car that they had was a well-designed auto, but not profitable. Mr. Whiting was getting old and wanted to retire, but had a company that was in debt. Along came Mr. Durant, who was greeted with wide-open arms and bought the wagon works for a $200,000 promissory note, assuming all debts, land, buildings, unfinished cars, wagons, axles, wheels, and all.

Billy was now on an acquisition hunt as had been his habit in years past, looking for the right car, the right proposition, the right path to follow, right or wrong. He was feeling whole again and life had meaning. His energy knew no bounds. In a matter of days after his recent accoutrements, he contacted Arthur C. Mason, who had built engines for Buick from the start and told him to organize a company and set up shop in the Flint Wagon

Winners and Losers

Works. Charles M. Begole and William S. Ballinger, who was associated with Whiting, were used by Durant in a new company called the Little Motor Car Company. This car would fill the niche that was opened when GM eliminated the Model 10, a small car that would compete with Ford's Model T. On November 3rd, 1911, the Chevrolet Motor Car Company was incorporated and yet another household name was born.

Chevrolet 1910

Billy's salesmanship now kicked into high gear. He opened a small factory in New York. Officers and friends queried, "Why?" Billy went on to extoll the virtues of having a centrally located showroom, where the center of commerce took place. It would be an excellent location, not only for domestic buyers, but also international purchasers and principals of other manufacturers. There, they could compare the features of Chevrolet to other—what Durant felt were inferior makes—from other auto manufacturers.

While that was going on in the east, Billy was grabbing up companies in Michigan and putting them under the Chevrolet

Corporation imprimatur. In the meantime, the Durant-Dort partnership of 27 years fell apart. The exact reason is not known, but in my estimation, Dort probably felt that Billy was heading down the same old road of too many irons in the fire. Chevrolet's credit was so bad in the early years that they had to use the Little Motor Car Company to order parts.

Charles Nash, one of Billy's early discoveries, settled in with GM very comfortably as its president, largely because of a man he brought in by the name of Walter Chrysler, who had abilities that were beyond what anyone's expectations were. The two of them, with their engineering and organizational skills, made GM into a smooth, profitable powerhouse.

By 1914, Chevrolet had introduced its overhead valve engine, now, everything was coming together for the Durant organization, but Louis Chevrolet's dream was coming apart. His penchant for building luxury cars met head-on with Billy's philosophy of a smaller, well-built auto that would compete in the lower end of the price scale. What Billy wanted to do was to have a high production auto that would meet the competition of Ford and GM. He was looking for the type of volume that would be impressive when he went to retrieve GM. By 1914, Billy felt that he could produce twenty-five thousand autos in that year, Hardy, an officer in the company, said that was impossible. As the one person Billy could rely on to tell him the truth, even if it was not what he wanted to hear, in discussing this further with him, they determined that to meet what they felt was a production goal, much more capital would be needed.

Since Billy's unpleasant and disgusting experiences at GM, he wanted nothing to do with bankers. Now, he was in a position where he would have to violate his own rule. Yet, he could be a little flexible when his principles interfered with his ultimate goal of reclaiming GM.

As related by Durant in his memoir: "I discussed the proposition with Mr. Nathan Hofheimer, who at the time did not have much money (Later, as a result of his association with me, he left an estate of $30 million). He had a number of influential friends, one in particular, L. J. Kaufman, president of the Chatham & Phoenix group of national banks. Hofheimer asked how much I could pay for the additional capital. I told him $5 per car for every car built over twenty cars a day. As a result of this offer, he arranged a meeting with Mr. Kaufman at his apartment in Ritz-Carleton Hotel.

"Because I had never met Mr. Kaufman and wished to have a friend in the event of our discussing a production proposal, I took with me Mr. A. B. C. Hardy, who was familiar with my many operations and proved a great help to me in many of the deals that I had put through at the time. During the conversation, Mr. Kaufman asked me, 'How much money can you use?' to which I replied, 'I could use the entire amount controlled by all of the Chatham & Phoenix Banks.' The discussion that followed led to the deal in which Mr. Kaufman's institution became interested in the enterprise and the leading financial influence in the development of the Chevrolet."

Kaufman agreed to take up the matter with Hornblower & Weeks, a well-known broker. They underwrote a stock issue that provided Chevrolet with $2,750,000. This was enough capital to swing the company into full production and started Chevrolet's hugely successful growth that propelled Billy back to the top of GM.

Chevrolet was now opening and franchising dealer-ships across the country, so it was necessary to open a production facility in California. Canada also started an organization under the auspices of Durant.

∞∂∞

In 1916, sales of cars and trucks was hitting a seventy-thousand mark, which was very impressive considering the year before they had only completed about fourteen-thousand. The growth was now phenomenal, but Billy was, of course, getting into the same onerous situation that he had spent most of his life contending with, namely, heavy burdens of debt. Of course, this did not stop old Billy from acquiring new avenues of debt by buying other companies that had something that Billy thought he could use—patents, new inventions, better engines, or a supplier of parts that may become useful to him in some way—even though the usefulness of these things did not seem evident at first. His quest for GM had not been quenched, and until it was, he would not stop expanding until Chevrolet was potentially on the same page as GM.

General Motors 1913

The Epic Battle for General Motors

Now the game began in earnest. Operating out of a suite of three rooms in the Belmont Hotel in New York City, with plenty of phones in each room, Billy enlisted trusted lieutenants to work the necessary contacts by phone. He had already enticed the captains of the world of finance and industry to buy as much of GM stock as they could manage. The most important giants were: Louis J. Kaufman, president of the Chatham & Phoenix Bank, Pierre S. DuPont, president of E. I. Du Pont de Nemours & Company and John K. Raskob, treasurer of the Du Pont Company, all of whom combined to form a syndicate to purchase GM stock very quietly, while GM was selling at a low premium to its intrinsic value. The stock was very much undervalued, because of the bankers' reticence to be aggressive in expanding the company, in order to protect what was owed to them, plus their commissions. They had never declared a dividend, though it could easily have been done. Their view of the auto industry was stilted, much like their bearing in everyday life; hence the seeds of their demise, at least in the auto industry had been sowed. Durant would see to that.

The work had just begun. The phones would be put to use calling the many thousands of friends who Billy had across the country, asking them to buy GM stock and hold the stock in trust for him until the September 16, 1915 stockholders meeting was to take place. At that time, he would gather together all the stock he could find and present it to the officers who would be presiding at the meeting. As the time grew short and the meeting neared, Billy redoubled his efforts and drove the people working for him nearly to complete collapse. Billy looked frazzled and close to a nervous breakdown himself.

This was to be the crowning achievement of his life, the pinnacle, the highest point of Mount Everest. Now was the time to gather all of his strengths, all of his considerable skills, and move with the cunning of a cat. He knew when he walked into that den of what he considered thieves, he would be the coolest, calmest predator of them all when he laid out the considerable stacks of stocks, certificates, and powers of attorney giving him the right to vote their stock as he saw fit.

The board was not in the dark and it was no surprise to them when Billy strode into the conference room wearing the brightest smile and a swagger that would have made General Patton proud. With his easy manner and his vice-presidential authority—remember, he still held the office of Vice President at GM—he asked to be recognized. With a grand, regal flourish, he deposited the stock that gave him control of GM into the treasurer's hands. Even though he acted in great confidence, secretly he was not sure he had enough stock. He endeavored to address the board and stockholders and gave them assurances that he held no vindictiveness in his heart; everything that he would do from that point would be to make GM a better company and position it for the future where every family would own an automobile. What he did not say was that the company would be a heap better off when he was able to excommunicate the bankers from the board of directors.

Eventually, a dispute developed between the bankers' faction and Billy. It was finally resolved when the bankers decided to allow DuPont to select three neutral directors. The bankers took this as an opportunity to curry favor with DuPont interests considering the amount of power they had in financial circles. It would prove to be a mistake, since DuPont's leaning was to Billy where they had just made a huge amount of money betting on him.

At the very next meeting, to the surprise of everyone, Durant was able to maneuver enough GM stock to the Chevrolet Corporation, and have Chevrolet gobble them up. This led to the dismissal of the banker's directorship. Durant was now able to accomplish what he had set out to do some years before. The immense satisfaction that he felt could not be contained and he celebrated by taking his wife out to a fast food restaurant for dinner. She asked why they had not selected a better place. Billy responded by asking if she was dissatisfied with the food. The disgusted expression on her face was such that Billy decided to change the conversation. No fool he.

∞∂∞

Charles Nash owed his rise in the automobile business to Durant, he became president of GM and sided with the bankers against Billy. After Billy gained control of GM, he decided to oust Nash. This was a course of action Billy was loath to pursue. Nash was a very able administrator and ran a tight ship, but he had to face the fact that Nash was a turncoat and could never again be trusted. However, in the matter of Walter Chrysler,

Winners and Losers

second in command, a man Billy very much wanted to keep, he proceeded to offer Chrysler a generous salary incentive. Chrysler, who wanted to start a company of his own, decided to accept Billy's over-the-top offer. Eventually, GM was reorganized and Chevrolet, the company that had swallowed GM whole, became just a subsidiary, one of the divisions of GM.

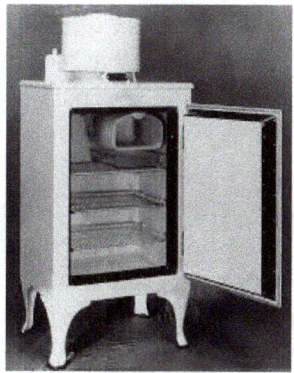

Frigidaire

In 1915 a new invention was being created by two men, Alfred Mellowes and Reuben Bechtold, working in their backyard. It was an electric cooling device. Many names were suggested, Cool Aid, Northern Lights, Jack Frost, and finally, the Guardian Refrigerator Company was selected, as proposed by their lawyer. As I look back on this new creation, it is my thought, how could it miss? Up to this time most people were using iceboxes, and in the winter, they used windowsills to store milk, cheese, butter, and other perishables. I can still remember as a child, stealing ice from the ice trucks on a hot summer day. It was no big deal and the driver rarely reprimanded us. I think he secretly empathized with us. We were just kids, having fun.

Mellowes and Bechtold incorporated the Guardian Company in March, 1916 and sold thirty-four refrigerators between 1916 and the spring of 1918. The small refrigerator company was deep in debt, but they finally were able to interest J. W. Murray of the Murray Manufacturing Co. in making an investment. However, the small company continued to lose money, due to production problems and for being underfunded.

 Durant heard about this little jewel through Murray and instantly realized the possibilities of this new and exciting invention. Of course, he personally bought a controlling interest in the Guardian Company. He set the company up in a larger factory, allowing production goals that they had never dreamed about. Durant was the person that came up with the name Frigidaire and eventually made it a part of GM. When the deal with GM took place, he never made a dime off the transaction.

∞∂∞

DuPont and Raskob, directors on the GM board, became deeply concerned in late 1916 about Durant ignoring DuPont, who held large chunks of GM and Chevrolet stock, and going about the affairs of his company in an imperious and arrogant way, without DuPont's council. Now, however, the U. S. became involved in the war in Europe, and things were rapidly changing. One thing that happened was that GM's stock had dropped from an eye-popping $200 to about $75. This inexplicable drop caused major problems for Durant the gambler, who had leveraged his large holdings of stock on a ten-percent margin and was receiving panic calls from his brokers requesting support of his margin. He got together with Raskob and explained his financial problems. Raskob, who was an officer in the DuPont Company, immediately brought in Pierre DuPont, who at this time was up to his ears in the affairs of the DuPont Company which, because of the war, was bringing in record profits. They decided to give Billy a salary of $500,000 a year, payable in advance, but this turned out to be insufficient. DuPont decided to pump $25,000,000 into GM's stock to support its price. He then created an executive committee, composed of Raskob and Durant, both gamblers and wielding the same power.

GM started on a massive buying campaign that led to the point that would eventually bring Billy into deja vue territory. Billy decided that there was a future in farm equipment, but not as big a future as he thought, resulting in a loss of $30,000,000.

∞∂∞

The Stock Market was always a big attraction for Billy. It provided him with all the action he wanted, so he spent less and less time in his business and more and more time playing the market. With his undisciplined method of operation, he was starting to piss off his best and most trusted lieutenants. It was standard operating procedure for Billy to keep them waiting for hours while he attended to more important matters, such as checking the price of a stock or buying and selling various positions in the market. He had this unfettered ability to concentrate on small details to the detriment of the larger picture and this alone was enough to send his associates into paroxysm of anger. At this time, Billy's arrogance came to the forefront. He would sit in a barber's chair he had installed in his office, while his barber worked on him, Billy would hold court.

This was not Billy's style and I believe that he had worked himself into such a frenzy, always in a hurry, that he did it just to save time. His officers and directors on the board did not understand it that way, and one by one, they started leaving Durant's employ. After all, these were highly skilled and competent employees and Billy was treating them as underlings with no real status in the company. Some who left started their own companies and became direct competitors. Two names that come to mind, Nash and Chrysler, would cause Billy to rue the day they parted ways.

I don't think it was in Durant's nature to ever look back, not his schtick. He only looked in one direction, forward and it would be the fly in the ointment that would cause Billy's demise.

∞∂∞

1919 would prove to be a watershed year and the expansion of

GM went on without any brakes. Where did the money come from? They created their own money by diluting the stock of the company. They issued stock that, in reality, did not exist, accomplished in two ways. The first is by declaring a stock dividend. Let's assume you own one-hundred shares. If the company declares a one-hundred percent stock dividend, you now own two-hundred shares. Of course, the value of the company would not increase, but the psychological effect would cause the value of the stock to increase, just as a stock split does today. The second way is issuing debentures or bonds with a stated interest rate, placing the company deeper in debt, but, on the other side of the ledger, the assets acquired with this new money theoretically increased the value of the company. Again, let's assume that the XYZ Company was acquired for $20,000,000 through a combination of debentures and stock. This now became an asset. But, if XYZ started losing money, it became just another drag on GM. Unfortunately too many of these entities were going down the proverbial tube at the same time.

1920 proved to be the undoing of many fortunes, especially those that tried to support the market in GM stock. As the stock declined, Billy with his natural inclination toward optimism, continued to buy more. In searching about for villains, he called Raskob to find out if any of the syndicate, meaning DuPont and the bankers were selling GM., Raskob told him he did not think they were selling but they felt the stock would decline further and this was not the proper time to purchase more stock. If Billy believed that these very astute men were not selling, then he was the worst kind of fool. I prefer to think that Billy's natural instinct was to believe in people and human nature, to his detriment. Billy continued to try to support GM with everything he had, including a $1,300,000 loan he received from the DuPont interests.

Sloan, the V. P. of GM, was considering resigning and went to Europe for a much-needed rest. When he got back he had

Winners and Losers

every intention of resigning, but it looked like things were coming to a head. He elected to stay until he could ascertain whether Billy would be receiving his pink slip or not.

The board was rapidly becoming extremely concerned about Billy's mounting debt load. They knew that if Billy had to go into bankruptcy, it would be the end of several banks that DuPont had heavy interests in. A meeting was proposed over Billy's vigorous protests; he kept insisting that there was nothing wrong. Eventually the meeting took place, and in an all-nighter, they found that Billy was $20,000,000 in over his head. It was finally agreed that DuPont would buy Billy's debt with something left over.

Billy knew it was game, set, match, and further protestations did not emanate from him. It was later indicated that he took it quite calmly. I tend to believe that he finally decided that the fight for GM was over and the equanimity he showed was an indication of his complete defeat and the utter destruction he felt to the depths of his soul.

Billy picked himself up, put the various parts of his person back together, and went looking for acquisitions. He was still with some amount of capital, and because of the great amount of goodwill he had achieved over the years, especially the goodwill he had achieved in Flint, Michigan. Billy's predilection to return to his roots in every stage of his life transformed Flint into the motor capital of the country. From a sleepy village of about five-thousand on the way to Detroit, to a bustling metropolis of over one-hundred thousand. Flint's favorite son made sure that Flint always played a role in his plans and they would step up once again in the new plans he was formulating.

Many times, the citizens of this enterprising city held awards dinners, presenting Billy with the keys to the city. But, as with everything that lives and dies, Mr. Durant has been largely forgotten. A statue was erected in the 1980s in a forlorn part of the city. He was a man that Flint and the country should never forget. His name should live in the annals of every grade school, high school, and college across this land, an echo of his spirit that should never die.

∞∂∞

Durant, with his energies revived, was once again thinking of a new venture that would completely blow away anything he had ever done. It was a new automobile to be called the "Durant." After all, cars were his business.

The Durant

Incorporation of the new venture got underway in earnest in 1920, barely six weeks after one of the greatest disappointments of his life. Bringing his salesmanship and genius to the forefront and once again selling stocks, bonds and swinging loans, he was now wheeling and dealing like his former days. The problem was he had nobody around like a Dort, or a Sloan, or a Chrysler. He was surrounded by yes men, and consequently, the brakes were never applied.

Dealerships and factories were established across the country and other car companies were acquired and absorbed by Durant Motors. New models of automobiles were created: the Durant Six, the Star. He acquired the Locomobile Company and other cars were in the planning stage. The stock of Durant Motors soared, but the company did not turn a profit. Finally, a media sage took notice of this situation and started to blow the whistle on the whole operation.

B. C. Forbes, a financial writer for the *New York American*, asked Durant if he was stripped of his fortune and in debt when he left GM, how could he finance the creation of a new company only six weeks later? Forbes wrote that Durant Motors' balance sheet in 1923 had as its largest asset $23.4 million, itemized as "participating contracts." Forbes explained that Durant formed two companies, Durant Motors and Star Motors, had them make contracts with each other, making these contracts an immediate asset worth more than $20 million. When you knew how, it was delightfully easy to make money on paper. He loudly proclaimed how Durant could justify a price of $80 on stock in a company that was losing money. Durant replied that, in a free market, many times it was a company's potential and the pressure of more buyers than sellers that determined a securities price.

The general tone of this commentary may have been meant to indicate that Billy was involved in a self-enrichment scheme, but Forbes would later recant this general indictment of Billy and went on to say that he had never heard in all the years he had been covering him, that Billy was in business for self-enrichment. I believe the Forbes rendition on Durant Motors was a watershed moment in the Durant saga.

∞∂∞

Even though Durant had been dealing in the Stock Market for many years, it now became an all-consuming passion, much to the chagrin of the officers and stockholders of his company. He formed a powerful consortium with the Fisher Brothers of Fisher Body fame and brought in other formidable investors. During the Twenties, they held a pretty tight rein on the market, their modus operandi a rather simple one. Billy was never one to care for the fundamentals of a company; this had showed in many acquisitions of companies that did not deserve their exalted price. He looked for companies that had a rather severe price decline, and would purchase their stock with impressive and breathtaking amounts of capital provided by the syndicate. This naturally drove up the price of the stock. Once they had made what amounted to a substantial profit, they would begin a rather complicated liquidation process that involved the ability to sustain the value of the security until they got out of that particular position.

At this period, Billy was living high, wide, and handsome. He had a luxurious estate in Deal, New Jersey, and other homes in New York, Florida and other far-away places, not to mention about ten automobiles. He spared no expense in furnishing these homes with antiques and artwork that was the envy of his peers.

One of the pretentious and ostentatious showings of his wealth was his own private railroad car. This memento gave him the ability to show how strong his influence on the securities markets was. Billy boarded his luxurious railroad car in New York and was proceeding southward to Florida. His rail car was parked on a siding when a train that was misguided inadvertently slammed into Durant's car, causing significant damage, not only to Durant's transportation but to other cars parked on the siding. At least two deaths and as many as 30 people were injured. Durant had injuries that at first were reported to have been major but proved to be something less than they had feared.

Markets sold off strongly when reports of Durant's injuries were exaggerated. Durant being Durant, he immediately started buying as soon as he could reach a telephone. This would prove to be prescient and Durant added to his already extensive fortune.

In 1929 he learned that the Federal Reserve would be restricting credit. By this time Billy considered himself to be an economic pro and he fought back at this indiscretion by the Fed. He called President Hoover and received an appointment. But his consultation with the President did not go well. He pleaded with Hoover that this action would cause interest rates to soar and just as in other times in the past when the market felt restricted from ready cash would be in a downward move. Hoover's feelings did not agree with Billy's assessment. Hoover informed him the market was overheated and it was time to reel it in.

After this meeting Billy decided to sell as many stocks as he could except for one investment that he was reluctant to sell. "Durant Motors." It was in his mind that selling the stock would hurt the stockholders who had bought into the company on his advice. This was just delaying the inevitable. In 1933 the company was declared insolvent and went bankrupt. In actuality the stockholders would have received more for their stock in 1929 than they finally ended up with.

It was during this time Billy discovered Europe, and together with his wife, took many trips to Europe while Durant Motors languished. Billy did try to revive the motorcar company at one time, but it was too late, because of his prior inattention to a company that could have been an unqualified success. The economy and executives who were lacking in the skills to run and organize a company of that size, caused it eventually to go bottoms up.

His company preceded Billy's bankruptcy, but not by much. During the early Thirties, sure that this market would turn around as it had always done in the past, he tried with all the resources he had to support the financial markets by buying stocks of substantial companies that he believed were undervalued, but to no avail. The warning that you receive in every prospective, or projection that some seer churns out, the small words in the document will tell you that the past is not indicative of the future. Truer words were never spoken. The market continued to decline.

Billy finally turned to his wife, Cathy, who was holding some 350,000 shares of GM that he had bought for her making sure that she would always have something if anything should happen to him. He went to her, hat in hand, and asked her for the shares, and she gave them to him without a moment's hesitation.

"Billy," she told him, "they are yours, and if there is anything else that I can do, I will. Without you, I never would have enjoyed the life we have lived up to now. I respect and have confidence in everything you do now, and forever more.

Billy was desperate, and with much self-loathing, took the shares and lost that too. In 1938, he was finally forced to sell his palatial estate along with the many accoutrements such as priceless oils that were one of a kind, silver sets along with expensive china, and numerous other things. He received a

Winners and Losers

pittance of $111,000 dollars. Most men experiencing this in that manner might have wanted to end it much like Jesse Livermore did when he killed himself after losing $100,000,000 dollars in the Depression. Billy, however, was of a different ilk. His optimism was so great that he truly believed he could make it all back. The problem with that thinking: you eventually run out of time, as all people do. We cannot live forever.

Billy Durant's judgment was not always correct in many things. Going into World War II, he put himself on the side of the pacifists, such as Charles Lindbergh, and in his later years, he expounded at length on the many errors of judgment he had made.

Undeterred by past failures, he proceeded to open up a bowling alley in Flint, Michigan with a drive-in diner next to it. This was located just a short distance from a giant GM plant that Billy had a hand in building. In fact, his initials were stamped in many of the bricks.

Yet, this was not just a bowling alley; this was Billy's new beginning, his resurrection as a potential behemoth in business once again. He envisioned bowling centers across the nation, along with drive-in hamburger havens. Those of you who can still remember the years after the war would recognize that his vision was absolutely correct. We had bowling alleys by the hundreds and drive in restaurants by the thousands and that may be an understatement.

∞∂∞

Billy's time on this earth was drawing to a close. One morning in his room at the Durant Hotel, he suffered a stroke and suddenly his dreams became null and void. He ended up back in New York at his home, and his one ambition was to return to his beloved Flint. He never made it. In March, 1947, Mr. William Crapo Durant passed away. He went, as we all must, in his case without a blazing epitaph, without a grand gesture, or an utterance of some declaration that we all could hold close to our hearts to be inspired by, and to have and hold for the rest of our

Ron Chicone

lives. There was none of that. The man who gave us an age that changed, not only the way we lived, but also the very landscape of our country with bridges, and highways that go from coast to coast, to every hamlet in the country …
Simply, quietly, expired.

The Future

One for the Road

A Story of Wickedness, Astonishing Courage and Destiny. A Woman for the Ages

Mary Lou Ambrose & Companion

Success is not in the genes. It has to be earned, but in what way? The path to riches is not strewn with rose petals, nor is it littered with thorns. Can we race along this path as if we are floating on a cloud, or must we stagger and bitch and leave footprints in blood, showing the wear and tear of the struggle?

∞∂∞

Mary Lou Ambrose awoke to the incessant ringing of the alarm clock. Hauling her bulk out of bed, she staggered into the bedrooms where her children slept, and started the process of trying to get them off to school, every morning, an arduous task. Then, back to her bedroom to confront a cantankerous husband who was possessive and controlling and get him off to work. Hopefully, tonight, he would bring the paycheck home. Would it not be wonderful if he took her out for dinner every now and then? She knew that would not happen. He never took her out, always afraid another man may look at her. Why they would was beyond her. When he arrived home that evening, his mood, at best, would be mercurial, at worst, surly. Mary Lou was completely overwhelmed with the many problems that confronted her every day of her life, a never ending procession, with an overly possessive and controlling man who constantly put her down, and complained about everything she did. This contributed to the desperation she felt on this particular morning. Now, with frustration, she hollered at the kids to get out of bed and they, as yet, had made no effort to stir. Eventually, the hollering turned into screaming, which brought a response from her husband.

"Jesus Christ, shut the fuck up, you goddam whore. Where in the shit were you when I got home last night?"

Her husband was by no means a little guy. He had a large frame, and ham-fisted hands. His face had no distinguishing marks, but carried a scowl that made his eyes look unusually small and beady. She was usually in a state of fear when he started ranting and raving. She rushed to placate this bear of a man, fearing his unreasonable anger would erupt into physical abuse.

"Danny, please, you know I was next door playing cards with Dorothy as I am every Thursday night."

"I can tell you right now, that shit is going to stop. You think I don't know you are using that card playing shit to cover up the fact you are sliding out of the house to meet somebody?"

"Danny, I have three kids to worry about. Do you think I'm stupid enough to run around with some other guy? Besides take a look at me. Who in their right mind would want me?"

After yet another morning of mind-altering episodes, she dragged herself through breakfast, the kids went to school, the bear went to work, and now, all was quiet, which gave her time to reflect on her life, and what she had become since the heady days when she was first married. Life seemed so simple, then. She would be the housewife she always wanted to be, have a bunch of kids and become a part of a loving family, but no sir-ee bob, it did not work out that way.

Making her way to the full-length mirror on the back of the bedroom door, she completely undressed and viewed her image. "Ugh!" she did not like—not even one little bit—what she saw. A body, bulky in all the wrong places. Her blue eyes, still the blue she had as a teenager, now had a downward tilt, not the uplifting tilt she use to have. An oval-shaped face that, at one time, was attractive, now looked puffy, and had the beginnings of a double chin. Her height, impressive in a good way, unfortunately was coupled with scraggly, short brown, nondescript hair that had no redeeming value. She inherently knew that, if she worked on getting her body into shape and falling into the hands of a talented hairdresser—whom she had not a pence to pay her with—she could still attract men.

Plunking herself naked on the edge of the bed, she thought about her life. *For God sakes, is this all there is. There has to be more than this. What in the hell can I do? Where can I go? Jesus God, I have three kids! If I leave now, I have no money, no job, and no car. I can't just leave, and desert my children, leaving them in the care of an abusive father.*

As she tried to get her thoughts in some semblance of order, events cascaded in and crushed her. She could go to the city's refuge for battered women, but the thought of being thrown together with other distressed females did not appeal to her. The choice of last resort would be her mother, but how would her mom feel about her daughter and three kids invading her in her fading years? Mary Lou had tried to shelter her mother all these many years, from the torment she had undergone with her husband. Always putting on a brave face and outright lying to her, she nevertheless suspected that her mother knew, as mothers usually do, what Mary Lou was going through, but trying to put it out of her mind, hoping for the best.

Mary Lou recognized that today would be the day, it was now or never. On this day she would take up the gauntlet and abscond with the children. Calling her mother with the vexing news she was leaving her husband and needed a place to stay, made Mary Lou faint with anxiety. Her last hope was her mother being receptive to taking her and the kids into her home until Mary Lou was able to get a job and have enough wherewithal to rent a place of her own.

Her mother was more than willing to do what she could.

Women are Heroines

I, as an author and onlooker of the human race, am appalled at the number of women who are abused, abandoned, and given insufficient child support, if at all. Yet, most of them go on to somehow establish a future life for themselves and their children.

Mary Lou had a hidden side that was tougher, than even she knew, true of most women I have known. It was not long before Mary Lou had won her way into a financial firm and became a secretary intimately involved in handling personnel matters. Having a job with some amount of remuneration on a regular basis, enabled her to provide the much-needed repair of her personal self.

The first chore was to entertain a strict diet, the second paralleling the first, changing her mousy brown hair for a startling, platinum blonde coiffure and letting it grow to shoulder length. The third chore became the selection of a completely different wardrobe. She did this with a personality that was changing dramatically, becoming bolder and more self-confident. Seeking out qualified friends and acquaintances, she sought as much advice as she could get, all of this done to the accompaniment of many threats and recriminations by her soon to be ex-husband. Yet, withstanding this assault proved she had the right stuff to make her own way in life.

Life for Mary Lou was turning around in a dramatic way, and she made a decision which would increase her income and point her in a direction better suited for her new image. Real Estate proved the classic profession for a person with the qualities Mary Lou possessed: toughness, a high-octane persona, good looks, and a recently made over body she loved to show off.

She dearly loved to show the new person she had become, and her passion took her to the many nightclubs that Cleveland possessed. In the divorce agreement, as a sop to her demands, her ex-husband gave up his fifty- percent interest in a small paint operation that had never made a cent. The other half of the ownership involved his cousin. Together they owned another business that seemed to make a little money. Unbeknownst to Mary Lou, they used this small business operation to siphon money to other interests they both owned. Mary Lou realized after a period of time that she had not received a stipend from this operation. On top of that, she received a notice from the Internal Revenue Service; she would be held personally responsible for thousands of dollars in back taxes. She decided to investigate.

Actually, she didn't have the slightest passion for this business, not even a little bit. She did, however, have a deep, all abiding passion for money. She had seldom visited this business, called

Painting Technologies, located in a suburb of Cleveland called Euclid. One morning she made the trip in a secondhand car with four doors, which she tried to keep in as nice a condition as was humanly possible. The car—a large model out of fashion and a little elderly—was needed to accommodate clients in the real estate business. Arriving unannounced, she encountered a pothole-filled, gravel road leading to a rusty building. Over the door, a sign announced that this was where Painting Technologies resided. She trudged up the gravel path and with some effort, pushed open the heavy metal door, encountering a dimly lit, cavernous interior with the odor of chemicals heavy in the air and made her way to what she thought was a working area. A black workman confronted her and asked what she wanted.

"Where the hell is the boss of this dump?" she demanded.
"You mean, John Ashby?"
"Yeah, I mean John Ashby."
"I am Lee Rolf. Who are you?" he responded.
"Lee, I am Mary Lou Ambrose, Danny's ex-wife, and in case you did not know, your other boss. I own half of this place."
"Oh, I see, I'm sorry I did not recognize you. John should be in any time now. He is probably having lunch. Can I show you around or make you comfortable until he gets back?"
"Yes, you can answer some questions about the operation of this place."
"Mary Lou, I just work here. I don't really know much."
"Tell me Lee, how many people beside you work here?"
"Me and two others."
"Where the hell are they?"
"Well, Mary Lou—"
"Forget Mary Lou, just call me M. L., okay?"
"The problem M. L, is the company does not have enough work, so we had to lay off those two guys."
"In your opinion, why do we not have more work?"

"I do not have any way of knowing what the problem is. Like I say, I only work here. Of course, I'm worried about my job."

John walked in, and seeing Mary Lou, walked up to her. "M. L., what brings you here today?"

"As you know John, I own fifty percent of this business, but I have not been kept informed of what the hell is going on here. I have not received any money and I have heard through the grapevine you intend to shut down this business. Is that true?"

"Yes, that's absolutely true. We do not have enough business coming in to justify all of the expenses."

"I suspect that we owe many people. Is that true?"

"Yes, that is also true."

Mary Lou, with rising anger, plied John with questions until she finally came to the most important one of them all. "I received a notification from the IRS that I owed them a considerable amount of money. Did you know that, John?"

Avoiding eye contact with Mary Lou, John just nodded his head.

Blazing words exited her mouth. "How did you two motherfuckers manage to get me involved in this bullshit? You two are going to hear a hell of a lot more from me. First of all, I will contact the bookkeeper, or accountant, or whatever he is called, and with a fine tooth comb, go over the books of this business and find out how much both of you have been stealing from me."

"Hold on M. L., I never intended to take anything away from you," John objected.

Mary Lou, feeling somewhat frustrated, said, "It has always been my experience; the person doing the protesting is generally the culprit. I believe the quote is, 'Methinks the gentleman doth protest too much.' My next project is to have a meeting with the IRS and find out who is responsible for this crap. One more question before I get the hell out of here. Have you as yet declared bankruptcy?"

"M. L., I am sorry you feel so distraught, but just imagine what I have been going through. My personal life has gone to hell and my wife is on the verge of leaving me. I have not filed for bankruptcy on this company, but I have on my other business."

"Goddamit John, I would like to feel sorry for you, but I have so many problems, yours looks insignificant to me."

Mary Lou was about to leave, and started walking to the door, when she suddenly whipped around, and grabbing John by the sleeve, said, "Listen to me. If we could come to some kind of an agreement, would you be amendable to me buying out your half of the business?"

"Hell yes, but you do not have any money. How is that going to work?"

She gathered herself up and said, "Look, buddy, where there's a will there's a way. I have the will; let me show you the way."

Mary Lou walked out, but could not get the business out of her mind. *I may be able to make a go of it if I could work something out with John,* she thought to herself. *I don't know a goddam thing about this painting business. I will need somebody to teach and direct me. I wonder how much that black guy, Lee, knows? He seems to be concerned about his job. I think he would be thrilled to have an opportunity to work with me, if he still had a paycheck coming in.*

Mary Lou called the accountant/bookkeeper as soon as she got home, and made an appointment to look over the books of Painting Technologies. After going over the books, she realized this was an exercise in futility. The amount owed by this business was, to put it nicely, excessive. However, she walked away with one excerpt from the books. They showed several checks were written from the bank account of Painting Technologies to the business owned by John and her ex-husband. This revelation gave Mary Lou a hammer to use in her efforts to get John to come to some understanding with her, concerning the purchase of his fifty percent of the business.

Connecting with the IRS and others, who were owed substantial sums of money, made Mary Lou realize that saving the business was damn near impossible, but, still, what the hell did she have to lose? She was already broke; how much more broke could she get?

Her next meeting with John went well. Using the sledgehammer of a possible lawsuit concerning the missing money, she coerced him into relinquishing his interest in the business for pie-in-the-sky future payments, if the company survived. Her next meeting was with Lee Rolf, apparently the only surviving employee of the company, who was willing to teach M. L. as much as he knew about the operation. This would prove to be a godsend in Mary Lou's future, which, at that moment, seemed rather dim.

The new venture would test two of Mary Lou's theories, developed while working in real estate. One was the theory of reality. "Maintain an assumption of success while expecting the worst possible result." This went along with her second theory concerning the law of averages. "Never mount an attack with a frontal assault. Always attack from the rear with, to use the Army term, an oblique invasion. Do this enough times, and you will be promoted to General of the Army, and be rewarded with much wampum."

As she took control of the company, she waded in with verve and feistiness. Her forte was predicated on the ability to maintain a personality of toughness, which allowed her to take the blows and keep coming back. These abilities came to the forefront as she called the various vendors and suppliers, requesting their indulgence in the matter of overdue payments. These people were not interested in more excuses, they wanted their money. Some had already turned what was owed over to bill collectors. The constant harassment by these collectors, contrary to what you might think, were not a distraction to Mary

Lou, but an opportunity to win them to her side with personality, professionalism and the promise that, given enough time, they would all get paid.

∞∂∞

A company's success is not only a reliance on the bottom-line, which is the amount you have earned, but first you must have a top line, or revenue. Without that, you have no bottom line. That was a reality that Mary Lou understood, so, she called and visited every person or company that had ever done business with her firm. Business started to pick up in a glacial way, but warming to a point where she brought the two employees that had been furloughed back to work.

This picture of Marylou Ambrose appeared in the Cleveland Illuminating Company Magazine, extolling her success in business.

Employees as of 2014. Painting Technologies

By dint of hard work, and sticking to the old-fashioned nose to the grindstone method, she was making the business work, but nose to the grindstone did not apply to her leisure hours. After years of being held down by a possessive and jealous husband, she wanted to taste it all. Married at a young age, she, consequently, never experienced the running around and craziness other girls indulged in. She also wanted to show off her new body, to make men squirm and yearn for more. Tight dresses or jeans along with high heels and low cut bodices—and hair that was a little tousled—were her modus operandi. One more thing also caused consternation; she was outspoken to the point of being abrasive. God help you if you were on the receiving end of one of her tongue-lashings.

It was against her nature to buy her own drinks. One of her ploys when entering a nightclub was to find a table with a number of men, introduce herself and announce that she was the social director. Then, selecting the least attractive man at the table, she would ask him to dance. It did not take long before she had plenty of other offers and all the drinks she could possibly want.

Most of the time, Mary Lou was prudent when drinking, but there were occasions when she went over her limits and all hell would break loose. She was asked to leave establishments more than once. Yet, most of the clubs actually welcomed her. She was generally good for business and caused the celebrants to enjoy themselves.

There were other times her antics were a cause for unintended consequences. An unforgettable evening in Myrtle Beach became etched in her mind, because it concerned a very prominent member of the federal government, one Strom Thurmond, a Senator and former candidate for President of the United States. While enjoying a well-deserved vacation with a close friend, she visited a popular restaurant and nightspot called "Sam Snead's." Mary Lou, as usual, searched and looked around to see what excitement she could stir up. Spotting a table with a full complement of men, she strolled over, and perceiving a gentleman well into geriatric age, she invited him to dance. He declined, but M. L. was insistent. Reluctantly, he got to his feet and started dancing with an overly exuberant Mary Lou. As the night wore on, she danced repeatedly with this elderly gentleman and urged him on to faster and faster dances, which he seemed to enjoy. Finally, he could no longer continue and begged off all future dances. It was not long before the contingent of men, including the elderly gentleman, took their leave and said goodnight to the ladies.

The next morning, she and her friend were listening to a television news station, when a flash was broadcast informing their audience that Strom Thurmond, the Senator from the State of South Carolina, was rushed to the hospital the previous night, suffering from cardiac arrest. He was one-hundred years old.

Mary Lou, after seeing a picture of Strom on TV, exclaimed, "Oh, shit! That's the old guy I made dance last night. Oh my God, I'm going to be blamed for killing Senator

Thurmond." As it turned out, Strom did make it past this crisis, only to pass away later because of old age.

Another memorable moment occurred when M. L. was arriving on a flight to Myrtle Beach. Her friend sent her male companion to greet her and get her settled in the condo she owned. He waited at the gate, and when she saw him her joy was boundless. Having just left the cold and general dreariness of Cleveland, her high spirits were understandable. Together they went to the baggage carousel, where the greeter, (the companion of her good friend) who will now be known as the Tortoise, received copious luggage. Mary Lou, as free as a bird, while he dragged the luggage and keeping up as best he could, proclaimed to one and all that the social director of Myrtle Beach had now arrived. As she passed a group of construction workers, she called out.

"You boys are sure looking good. I especially like those brogans you're wearing. Too bad I don't have more time or I would stay and socialize for a while, but, hey, I'll be at 2001 tonight and you are all invited."

2001 was a very popular nightspot that M. L. and her friends frequented in North Myrtle Beach.

On the way to the condo, she decided that her companion, the tired Tortoise and she, would stop for a welcoming libation. They entered the tavern and she straightaway made friends with the men sitting at the bar, informing them that the Tortoise following her was not with her; he was just her girlfriend's guy.

"Do not worry about him; the party is now on."

So many men, so little time.

∞∂∞

Winners and Losers

On another excursion to Myrtle Beach, a very troubling incident took place. Well, it would have been troubling, but, knowing M. L., it became laughable, strangely one part of an incident that cast derisiveness on a vacationing traveler from abroad and another part that cast aspersions on a flight attendant.

It seems she had a flight that had a lengthy stopover in Charlotte, North Carolina. Of course, Mary Lou, being the bon vivant, spent that time in the cocktail lounge enjoying the company of a few men experiencing the same inconvenience. After several drinks, provided by her new friends, a tipsy M. L. boarded the plane for the last part of the trip to Myrtle Beach. After boarding the aircraft, she was lucky enough to obtain a roomy seat arrangement, one that was the passageway to the emergency exit door. The gentleman sitting next to her appeared to be of Japanese background. Mary Lou, because of her past experience working and socializing with masculine men, could be deprecating in social situations requiring a certain amount of circumspection. When issuing words that could be interpreted as derogatory, she simply viewed them as just a laugh and not to be taken seriously.

The Flight Attendant came around and asked the gentleman sitting next to her in the window seat if he was physically capable of handling the exit door in the event of an emergency. He replied that he would be capable, if called upon. Upon hearing this, Mary Lou sat bolt upright.

"What the fuck are you talking about?" she said in a loud voice. "This Jap bastard's ancestors are the ones who bombed Pearl Harbor and killed thousands of Americans and you want to trust him to save our lives?"

The flummoxed attendant was taken completely by surprise, and weakly asked her not use such language.

"Kiss my ass," Mary Lou said in her inimitable way.

The attendant, completely beside herself, had other duties to perform, and for the moment allowed this latest outburst to go unchallenged. Later in the flight, Mary Lou became belligerent, demanding another drink. The flight attendant correctly refused, realizing she was intoxicated. As the repartee ensued, somewhere in there M. L. called the attendant a cunt. Having had enough, the flight attendant made her way directly to the cockpit and informed the pilot of the events that were occurring.

He sent the co-pilot to the passenger compartment to inform M. L. that, if her diatribe continued, he would have her placed in restraints. In the meantime, the pilot radioed Myrtle Beach Airport asking to have security personnel and the local police standing by for a possible arrest of an unruly passenger.

Standing at the gate where the passengers from Mary Lou's plane were to disembark, was M L's good friend, waiting to welcome her to Myrtle Beach. She waited and waited, until all the plane's passengers had left the aircraft. Finally, a passenger who had witnessed the entire incident approached her and asked if she was waiting for a blonde lady."

"Yes I am, do you know where she is?"

"She had a few problems on the flight, and at this time, is being held by the police on the plane."

"Oh, my God! What has she done now?"

The passenger went on to say that, in his opinion it was nothing and the airline was overreacting to a few blue words said to one of its employees.

M. L.'s friend waited until she emerged from the plane in the company of two Myrtle Beach police officers. She walked up to the officers and introduced herself, apologized for the actions of Mary Lou and said, "if they would release her, she would take her home and put her to bed."

"Officers, Mary Lou is really a very nice person, but just had too much to drink."

"We take these kinds of incidents very seriously. I hope that, in the future, there will be no obnoxiousness like the display she put on this afternoon. Get her sobered up and then give her a good lecture."

Mary Lou did not give up drinking entirely, but she was more respectful of airline employees thereafter.

Ron Chicone

Ocean Annie's

Let The Good Times Roll

Winners and Losers

One of the joys of living on the beach was the number of bars and clubs that lined the Grand Strand. Many of them were standalone oases and others were connected with the many hotels and tourist havens that existed along the Strand. A standout among the many palaces of joy was a place called Ocean Annie's.

On one particular night, Mary Lou came blustering in, and of course, was her usual effervescent self, proclaiming to all within earshot that she was the Mayor of Social Studies in Myrtle Beach and class was about to begin. What a class it was! As the evening progressed, and getting toward closing time, M, L, decided to put an exclamation point on the evening by doing a striptease. Not on the dance floor, or any other floor, but on one of the highest tables there.

Get this picture in mind. She had more than a couple of drinks and had danced every dance. That scenario was not a feature that led to legs—even though well-constructed—as the best base for a strip tease on a high tabletop. As she wobbled through a distressing disrobing, people were flooding into the bistro, coming from all over, even from the beach. The manager, completely discombobulated, was trying to make his way to her table as fast as he could find a way through the crowd. His worry was not the striptease, but the sanctions that the city might carry out against the club if it became public knowledge. The crowd, realizing what the manager was trying to do, formed a solid wall in front of him to impede his way, and delay the final triumph of this improbable exhibition. Mary Lou with wild enthusiasm, and great abandonment was getting down to the bare essentials, when a terrifying thought occurred to her, she could not remember the last time she had a Brazilian wax, so, consequently, she trimmed the strip tease, much to the disappointment of the cheering crowd.

The evening ended with M L and her friends enjoying many cocktails and other offers, some congratulations and others of the suggestive type and more than a little ribald. When the manager finally got to M. L., he indicated with a veiled wink of the eye that she would be forever banned from this establishment.

The next night, Mary Lou entered Ocean Annie's with a large contingent of friends and was welcomed with open arms, but informed that she could not, in any way, carry out the entertainment that evening. That was okay with her, for she was still tired from the night before.

Returning to Cleveland after a sojourn to the sunny Myrtle Beach was always a bit of a downer. When she entered the somewhat depressing building that her business occupied, she immediately had to change her personality from the bon vivant to a serious CEO who demanded respect. Coming down from these exciting vacations were always difficult, but, gradually, reality invaded her reverie, and before she knew it, she was into the challenges that her business called for.

Here are the points that Mary Lou adhered to in her rise to becoming exceedingly successful:

- Treat all employees as equals and with respect.

- Compensation for employees should be somewhat above industry average, with as much side benefits as the business can afford.

- Take a personal interest in the life of each employee.

- Treat all clients as close friends. Make them feel as if their problems are your problems.

- Keep records on all aspects of the organization, especially anything concerning the city, state, county, federal, or the IRS.

- Comply with all laws and licensing requests of any entity that has authority over the business.

- Above all, keep learning. Remember that every person has pearls of wisdom that can be imparted to you, and help not only your enterprise, but also yourself to become better.

An illustration of the evolution of Mary Lou came about when she was invited to a top-of-the-line wedding in one of the old mansions on Euclid Avenue, in Cleveland. It was a very exclusive event that encompassed much heraldry, pomp, and circumstance.

Euclid Avenue at one time was possibly the richest street in America, or possibly the world.

Excerpt from Wikipedia, Millionaire's Row

"In the second half of the 19th century and early in the 20th century, Euclid Avenue was internationally known. Baedeker's Travel Guides called the elm-lined avenue "The Showplace of America" and designated it as a must-see for travelers from Europe. The concentration of wealth was unparalleled; the tax valuation of the mansions along "the Avenue" far exceeded the valuation of New York's Fifth Avenue in the late 19th century. Accounts at the time compared it to the Avenue des Champs-Élysées in Paris and the Unter den Linden in Berlin.

Euclid Avenue was an elegant showcase for Cleveland's wealthy citizens, who built their grand mansions high on a ridge overlooking Lake Erie. Set two to five acres back from the avenue, which was paved with Medina sandstone, the mansions seemed to float amid spacious, landscaped grounds.

Families living along "Millionaire's Row" included those of John D. Rockefeller (during the period, 1868-84), Sylvester T. Everett, arc light inventor, Charles F. Brush, George Worthington, Horace Weddell, Marcus Hanna, Ambrose Swasey, Amasa Stone, John Hay (personal secretary to Abraham Lincoln and Secretary of State under William McKinley), Jeptha Wade (Cleveland benefactor and founder of Western Union Telegraph), Alfred Atmore Pope (iron industrialist and art collector), Worthy S. Streator (railroad baron, coal mine developer, and founder of the city of Streator, Illinois), and Charles Lathrop Pack.

Residence of Cassie Chadwick on Euclid Ave.

Euclid Avenue's most infamous resident was con artist Cassie Chadwick, the wife of

Dr. Leroy Chadwick, who was unaware that his wife was passing herself off to bankers as the illegitimate daughter of steel magnate Andrew Carnegie.

Cassie was probably one of the most prolific con artists in the late 1800's. Married multiple times and had professions ranging from fortuneteller, clairvoyant, and madam of a brothel. She borrowed from various people and banks in excess of five million dollars sending one bank into bankruptcy.

Winners and Losers

The incredible Mrs. Chadwick eventually was sent to the Ohio State Penitentiary, on March 10, 1905 and sentenced to fourteen years. She passed away in prison on her birthday Oct. 10, 1907 age 50.

Growth of Commercial District and Decline of Millionaire's Row

By the 1920s, the former "Millionaire's Row" was in decline. During the Great Depression, many mansions were converted by their owners into rooming houses, which accelerated the decline. In the 1950s, Cleveland's Inner-belt Freeway cut through Euclid Avenue, between downtown and the rail crossing at East 55th Street. By the 1960s, the street that once rivaled Fifth Avenue as the most expensive address in America was a two-mile (3 km) long slum of commercial buildings and substandard housing. In the late 1960s, Cleveland Cavaliers owner Nick Mileti announced plans to move the basketball club from Euclid Avenue's Cleveland Arena to a new arena in suburban Richfield Township."

The action by the Cleveland Cavaliers wrote the final chapter of Euclid Avenue.

University Club/Former Beckwith Mansion

One of these magnificent homes was restored and converted to an enterprise that held parties, weddings, and other get-togethers. On one fateful night, Mary Lou was invited to a wedding that was elegant in every way. She entered the mansion through massive oak doors, with her coterie of wannabe clones, attracting people like moths to a bright light. On this night, the ensemble was greeted and announced by two trumpeters and a butler, using replica heraldic trumpets from the days of the grand knights of England. Escorts led the way to their table for the evening, where cameras and a choice of wine preceded their presence. The dance floor was quite large and could accommodate the flowing dances of the day, played by an orchestra that was a reincarnation of Glenn Miller.

Needless to say, M. L. glimmered in a red sheath dress that flared out at the knees but left little to the imagination above that. Her hair, just a little tousled, and diamond earrings that emitted a cascade of sparkling lights, together with a diamond-studded belt that benefitted from the reflection of the vibrant red dress, left no doubt to the sexuality being emitted.

The evening became a montage of beautiful, artful displays of food and culinary delights that would have been a tribute to a Rembrandt painting. Much of this escaped Mary Lou. Her interest was centered on the well-stocked bar that occupied a copious amount of space in one of the beautiful rooms of the mansion. As it turned out, there just happened to be a grand column not too far from the bar. As M. L. perused this column, it looked to her as if it was an elegant pole, to be utilized in a way that, very possibly, Josephine Baker, one the world's first celebrities of dance, would have when she performed in Paris in 1925.

Winners and Losers

What went on in Mary Lou's head was far removed from the ordinary woman. She saw things in a kaleidoscope of images that gave wings to an imagination that flew above worldly concepts. The performance she embarked upon this night was just a little eerie. She caressed the column as if it was an imaginary lover, a great lover she never had.

The end of this fairy tale came when she looked up and realized one of her best customers was entering the room. The transformation that took place was immediate and complete. She became the model of decorum, rushed to his side, and escorted him and his wife to her table. The rest of the night would no longer include any further displays of dancing or drinking. This was business, the hell with dreaming; money came first and making her business number one was the agenda of the night, taking orders was the order of the evening, the kind that translated into scads of effervescent cash. Dollars were the thing that would turn her dreams into reality. Hell, with enough money she could travel to the Kasbah in Morocco, and dance to her heart's delight. The public relations she lavished on this customer on that magical night proved to be a godsend, as he and his company ranked among her biggest supporters.

Mary Lou's business grew exponentially as she expanded into government contracts after qualifying through strenuous exams. A fortuitous event occurred when, in the course of her partying, she met the gentleman that would become the very thing that made her life complete. Never one to sleep around, in fact discouraging anyone from an act of familiarity, such as touching her in a way that was obviously sexual in nature. When she met the man of her dreams, her sexual quotient exploded. Her happiness knew no bounds. Up to this point she had almost given up meeting anybody who would arouse in her a lust for life beyond the things that had become mundane. All of a sudden, her life took on a new quest. Bars, bistros, saloons, and nightclubs were now passé. Her horizons expanded. An interest in history and visits to areas that were formally not in her jargon, were now on her agenda. An interest in the game of golf became paramount, so, naturally, a visit to Augusta National Golf Course, during the Masters Golf Tournament, was imperative. What will follow is an absolutely true narrative of an incident that goes far beyond one's wildest dreams, the limited imagination of most people never reaching that far.

The Incident at
Augusta National Golf Course
During The Masters Golf Tournament

Her companion, who was an ardent golfer, had introduced M L to the game of golf and asked her if she would entertain the thought of a trip to Augusta, Georgia to watch one of the premier golf tournaments in the world. Mary Lou, by this time an ardent golfer herself, jumped at this suggestion. As a matter of fact, she had filled her home with everything golf, so no matter where you turned you ran into something that had to do with this game, a towel, a wall plague, a center piece for the coffee table, the carpet, bed sheets, on and on ad nauseam.

Obtaining tickets to the tournament was usually an act of futility, but, with enough money and/or connections it was possible. Her companion, having worked at the Fulton Market in Cleveland, knew the right people and was able to procure the required tickets. A joyous occasion was to be had by this couple who were madly in love. The expectations that were created by the newspapers and the sports writers, plus pictures of this famed place gave them an anticipation of standing on the precipice of an escarpment, where they could soar with the wings of eagles over the entire beautiful golf course, formerly the site of a nursery.

Love, if we can remember, is rapacious, irascible, fiery, or predatory, also magnificent, wonderful, greater than anything we have ever experienced. When in this state of the Promised Land, we can feel the blood coursing through our veins like a thundering herd. The things we are capable of doing during this period are truly amazing, though not approved of in the estimation of polite society. Of course, nearly everyone, at one time or another, exposes themselves to the ridicule and ramifications of society.

Much enjoyment had been propagated throughout the days of the tournament and Mary Lou was anxious to do something her companion would remember for the rest of his life. The contest was winding down and they were standing along the left side of the eighteenth fairway among a crowd of onlookers. Across the fairway was nothing but woods and the cottages that had been built to honor famous personages. Two that stood out were the Eisenhower and Bobby Jones cabins. As the fortunate last golfers passed by and made their way to the eighteenth green, taking the crowd with them, Mary Lou quietly, but firmly, took her boyfriend by the arm and propelled him across the fairway and into the woods. When they reached a place that seemed rather private. Mary Lou stopped, pushed him against one of the towering pines and kissed him passionately, then proceeded to overpoweringly entice her companion into an act of love.

Butler Cabin

18th Green & Sand Trap

He was unable to resist, even though a television crew was telecasting from one of the cabins. He was sure that one of the telecasters had a bird's eye view, but, this being the Masters, nobody wanted to report such a thing happening from those sacred grounds. So, depending on how you viewed this incident, it was either a sacrilege on pseudo-sacred ground, or a wonderful expression of love and passion. To make this sacrilege more complete, she took a personal item, that will forevermore remain a secret, from her and her lover, and when she was able, buried them in the sand trap in front of the eighteenth green. Never had this magnificent course been brought to its knees like that!

After this caper, M. L. settled down to a more tranquil life, visiting places that included the Golf Hall of Fame, John Ringling's home, Ca d'Zan in Sarasota, Saint Augustine in

Florida, Charleston, SC, along with other places that are historical in nature. Her business on the ascendancy allowed her and Bob to acquire a beautiful home on a golf course in Myrtle Beach.

This story could have never been accomplished without a never-ending desire to get ahead, regardless of the obstacles placed in her way. She had a fire in her belly that could not be quenched. Remember, when all seems hopeless, pull out Mary Lou's words to live by:

Where there's a will there's a way. I have the will; let me show you the way."

One of Three Homes She Owns

Amelia Earhart

Courage is the price that life exacts for granting peace.
The soul that knows it not knows no release.
From little things, knows not the livid loneliness of fear,
Nor mountain heights where bitter joy can hear,
The sound of wings.

How can life grant us boon of living, compensate?
For dull, gray ugliness and pregnant hate,
Unless we dare.

The soul's dominion? Each time we make a choice
We pay with courage to behold resistless day
And grant it fair.

Amelia Earhart

Fokker Tri Motor **Electra Cockpit** **Amelia**

Avro Avian

Amelia, the quintessential All-American Girl, what the girl next door should look like. Beautiful, demure smile, sleek figure, effervescent and pleasing personality, unselfish, boundless energy. Let me introduce an American legend. Amelia Earhart. Bigger than life itself. The forever young, forever-legendary aviatrix.

Amelia approached the ungainly looking aircraft gingerly. Her flying experience up to this time, in 1928, had been of a limited nature. There was no-way in hell she was capable of handling a three engine aircraft with powerful experimental, Whirlwind engines. Yet, she had been invited aboard this flight over the Atlantic to become the first female to make the crossing. Her trepidation was enhanced knowing two women the year before, in 1927, had tried and failed. One died and one was seriously injured.

Her personal comportment gave off the aura of being shy, self-deprecating and a bit on the reticent side. That was far from the truth. The nature she had always inwardly exhibited was, to put it mildly, a risk taker and just a bit on the careless and wild side. Not only was this evident in her flying efforts, but also in her amorous adventures. She had a view of life most youth have, *indestructible*, in her case it was apparent in her belief in her manifest destiny, which culminated in the conviction that women were the equal of men. She set out to prove just that, not in words, but in actions. Yet, the implications of this certitude would lead to her death.

Now, as she strode with her long lanky legs to this, what seemed to her a bulky blob of an airplane, she wondered what maleficent modifications were taking place on this flying machine. Amelia was not a participant in the many decisions taking place regarding this aircraft and she did feel a certain resentment she kept well bottled up.

The airplane bobbed up and down in East Harbor Bay, Boston. Unbeknownst to Amelia, pontoons replaced the wheels and this did not meet with her instinctive approval, since a seaplane had a much harder time gaining sufficient speed to become airborne. The pontoons characteristically stuck to the water, much like trying to pick up a wet dime. Add to this the immense amount of fuel required to transverse the Atlantic, plus the number of humans, a total of three, who would be on board with all the gear they needed to survive in the cold, high-altitude flight. In order to become airborne, a plane with pontoons installed needed just the right amount of sea swells and headwinds and had to attain an air speed of at least fifty-five miles per hour to lift off.

Charles Lindbergh, referred to as "Lucky Lindy," or the "Lone Eagle," had flown the Atlantic the year before, becoming the first aeronaut to traverse the Atlantic Ocean non-stop, with a single engine plane which was not equipped with pontoons. He felt, and later made it clear, pontoons would not be worth the added problems they would cause and Amelia tended to agree.

Amy Guest

Charles Lindbergh

George Putnam

Bill Stultz   **Hilton Railey**

The guiding lights behind this venture included Captain Hilton H. Railey, head of a public relations firm, and George Putnam, in publishing and promotion, a promoter par excellence, with shades of a huckster in his character. Mrs. Frederick Guest had the temerity to originate this undertaking, with the wherewithal to fund the venture. It was because of her family, the redoubtable Phipps's estate, which made it all possible. Formerly Amy Phipps, Mrs. Guest purchased the plane and named it "Friendship." This was done with an eye on the ultimate prize, herself as the pilot and the first woman to fly the Atlantic.

In her preparations for this transatlantic flight, she hired an excellent pilot, Wilmer "Bill" Stultz, who had a great amount of experience, and in fact, accompanied Admiral Byrd on his arctic sojourn. However, he had a predilection for excessive drinking, and in fact, he was a hopeless alcoholic. Amelia probably did not know about Bill's problem, and if she had, she would have refused to sign on for this venture. Her father had a problem most of his life with alcohol and this experience led Amelia to be a teetotaler all of her life.

Mrs. Guest's family intervened in Amy's foolish, and in their view, irrational decision to fly a transoceanic flight. Amy ceded to their fervent request and then turned to Hilton Railey, informing him of her decision. Amy decided she would continue funding this trek, but reserved the right to have the final say on the choice of the aviatrix they would finally settle on. The criteria she asked for was not very stringent, she would have to be intelligent, have completed the attainment of her pilot's license, be reasonably attractive and a person of high moral standards. Railey turned to a person he held in great esteem, retired Rear Admiral, Reginald R. Belknap. He immediately thought of a personable, young social worker, Amelia Earhart.

Railey and Putnam quickly scheduled her for an interview, and when Amelia was informed of her possible selection of the first woman to fly the Atlantic, her enthusiasm knew no bounds. The interview was held in Railey's office, accompanied by Putnam and Ms. Guest. Amelia burst into the room with unmitigated zest showing in every move she made. They asked her to make herself comfortable in one of the oversized armchairs, and even though she was slight of build, she seemed to fill the chair.

Amy was the first to speak. "My dear girl, what makes you think you have the courage and skill to make this historical flight?"

"Mrs. Guest," Amelia replied, "from the moment I became interested in flight, a passion developed in me to promote, not only aviation, but the advancement and equality of women as the equals of men. So, if I can create an interest by other women in this sphere, where I may acquire some influence, then I might be able to persuade many other females to follow my example".

"Well, that is all well and good, but do you realize other people have been injured and killed trying to accomplish this feat? In fact, two woman aviators have recently tried and failed. One was seriously injured and the other is now deceased."

Amelia leaned forward in her chair. "When attempting anything where you would be the first, risks will be abundant and I will be more than willing to be the one to face the hazards this will entail. But whether or not I survive is neither here nor there; it is possible I may be an inspiration to other women and will have advanced what I feel is my goal in life."

Putnam was immediately enchanted by her inexplicable presence, and immediately, he seized upon the attributes she exhibited, which were many. She kept a churlish, truculent, aggressive personality well hidden under an impish face and her native intelligence seemed to ooze out of every pore. Her attractiveness and quiet demeanor alluded to Charles Lindbergh, which Putnam realized would be money in the bank with the media and other forms of potential compensation, which he would trade on to achieve Amelia's conceivable fame.

Railey, on the other hand, was looking at other aspects of Amelia's attributes. One area he was particularly interested in was the ability to overcome obstacles of which he was sure would be many. It meant having the ability to analyze a situation and react in a cool, conservative, and level-headed, manner. Yet, he sensed in her an aggressiveness that might cause her to act in an impulsive fashion as opposed to a rational reaction to an impending problem.

Amy immediately felt a comradeship with Amelia. She loved her idealism concerning the future role of women in aviation. Amy continued the interview.

"Do you currently have any personal involvements at this time?"

"Yes I do. I have a friend I have been dating off and on for several months. If you are asking if my intentions are to make this a permanent arrangement, then I must answer in the negative."

"You know young lady," Railey said, "You will be in close proximity to two or three men in very close quarters. How will you handle the embarrassing hygienic aspects of the trip without having any privacy?"

"This is something I have not given much thought to and I can tell you I will not be embarrassed, but I wonder how the men will feel?"

Putnam now brought up a subject considered touchy indeed and nobody knew how Amelia would respond.

"It is my duty to inform you, if you are selected for this voyage, no recompense will be due you. However, if successful, I will see to it there will be substantial benefits accruing to you."

"If I may interject," Amelia cut in, "my intention in appearing for this interview was not to enrich myself, but to accept a challenge I am personally hungry for. God willing, if I return unscathed, it will be an uplifting experience to all woman all over the world. It matters not what becomes of me, because surely there will be others who will take up the sword."

After clearing a few more details, the meeting was adjourned. Amelia had made an impressive presentation and everyone felt she should be the one. No one was more impressed than George Putnam. First, he was somewhat of a lothario and her naturalness and beauty appealed to him. Second, he decided, somewhere in the future, he would approach her for more than just dinner. Before that could happen, however, he would try to make her more dependent on him for the notoriety he sensed she craved, assuming she survived the caper. After spending time with Miss Earhart, and observing her actions and responses, his enthusiasm was boundless. She was a reservoir of future wealth to him, and incidentally, to her. Yes, he was a wolf in sheep's clothing, and unbeknownst to her at the time, she would willingly and knowingly become the wolf's mate.

He had pegged her about right.

The Flight of the Friendship

While awaiting the epic flight to get under way, it was imperative for Putnam to keep Amelia under wraps. Gangs of newsmen, photographers, and paramount newsreel cameramen were trying to get interviews with her, but he and others were not ready to unwrap her just yet. One of the ruses they would employ when registering at a hotel was using Dorothy Putnam's maiden name, Binney, the wife of George Putnam, she was currently Amelia's close friend, and their relationship would be rent asunder with a measure of animosity in the future.

On Sunday, June 3, 1928, the Friendship waddled eastward, destination Trepassey, Newfoundland. Inclement weather interfered, but they landed in the harbor and were surrounded by hordes of people, since almost the whole population of Trepassey had turned out. From there they would take flight across the Atlantic and put down, God willing, in Ireland.

Trepassy   **20 Hours and Forty Minutes Later**

Inclement weather kept them grounded for an unreasonable amount of time. Other excursions over the Atlantic were forming, causing Amelia and the others a great amount of angst. Many dollars would disappear if they were not the first to make the trip. Because of these building pressures, tempers were becoming frayed.

On Sunday, June 17, the Friendship wobbled into the air bound for Europe, with a forecast of inclement weather ahead. Bill, however, had a paralyzing hangover, which greatly aggravated Amelia, and harsh words were spoken. Amelia had a fiery temper when provoked, and her use of adjectives not normally expressed by a well brought up lady tended to be explosive. As they ambled over to the Friendship airplane before takeoff, this conversation took place:

"Jesus Christ, Bill, you dumb son-of-a-bitch; you are doing everything in your power to fuck up this flight.

"Just a goddam minute, you skinny bitch. I'm in no mood to hear your holier-than-thou sermons. You act as if you are the complete triumvirate on this trip. Well you're not; you are only a passenger, just like a sack of potatoes."

"The only reason you got this expedition was because of me," Amelia responded. "Why don't you just sleep with a female instead of cozying up to that bottle at night? I suspect that thing between your legs does not work anymore, is that it? I've got news for you, come hell or high water, this plane will be in the air today, regardless of the poor weather reports, and whether you are at the controls or not. As far as I am concerned you can take a hike."

This exchange did nothing to relieve the tension between them. Luckily, the third person completing the aforementioned triad was Louis "Slim" Gordon, a very competent pilot and an extraordinary mechanic capable of flying the plane to its destination, should the need arise.

One of the stupidest things possible was to jettison gasoline to enable the plane to get airborne. Of the initial nine-hundred gallons, they dumped two-hundred of them, which enabled the plane to achieve flight, but only seven-hundred gallons of fuel remained, barely enough to reach the shores of Ireland, leaving no room for error. If they had waited a little longer, they would have had more favorable conditions, which would have enabled them to take off with a considerable amount more fuel. Yet, the pressure from George Putnam was intense. He was more than willing to risk lives in order to have Earhart be the first woman to cross the Atlantic.

As it turned out, they did miss Ireland, and after a considerable amount of apprehension, they were lucky to make the coast of Wales. Overall, it was a harrowing flight, lasting twenty hours and forty minutes.

Instant Adulation

A heroine was born and the world went crazy over a woman having crossed the Atlantic. Ticker tape parades, published books, speeches, appearances, and advertising contracts were now the order of the day and Putnam's ship, or should I say plane, had come in. Nevertheless, the whole ordeal was a disappointment to Amelia, as she really *did* feel she was simply a sack of potatoes on the excursion, only a mere passenger. At no time during that flight did she touch the controls and she tried to express that sentiment whenever she was asked, much to the chagrin of George Putnam. It mattered not, however, her whirlwind life was now in high gear. She was referred to as "Lucky *Lady* Lindy," a moniker applied by a columnist because of the physical resemblance between her and Lucky Lindy Lindbergh, both were slim, fair, lanky, and taciturn.

While still in Europe, accolades rained down on Amelia and their plane was torn apart by souvenir hunters, Amelia, Stultz, and Gordon arrived in New York to be honored by a ticker tape parade down Fifth Avenue. As she rode with her two fellow pilots, she realized the cheering and idolatry emanating from the spectators was primarily for her. George Putnam tried to enter one of the cars in the parade, as it was his practice to inject himself in every photo or platitude given Amelia, but, on this occasion, he was brazenly brushed aside. The Ticker Tape Parade was followed by an invitation from the "loquacious"

President of the United States, Calvin Coolidge, to attend an event held at the White House honoring the courageous flyers.

Entering the White House and being escorted by ramrod straight Marine guards, sent chills up her spine. It was a moment that would live in her mind, like a fairytale. How was it possible to believe for an instant that this could happen to her? Inwardly she felt she was still a little nothing from the heartland of America.

George Putnam, through Amelia's good graces, was able to attend, and as much as possible, draped himself all over the flower of the evening. He made sure photographs taken of Amelia included him. Aggressiveness was his hallmark, and if anything, did not endear him to many people. His mind was already working on the future promotions that would possibly come his way. For her part, the magic of the evening being spent holding a conversation with the President of the United States under the sparkling extravaganza of the chandeliers of the East Room of the White House, left her breathless.

Now the work began. G. P., as Amelia referred to George Putnam, had put together a five-city tour for her that included banquets and socials he requested she attend. More than that, he wanted her to stay at his home in Rye, New York, where, under his tutelage, she would start writing the book about the transatlantic flight, tentatively titled, *The Flight of the Friendship*. As soon as she had the opportunity, she took him aside with some amount of diffidence.

"George you have been talking about these grand plans for me, but I have yet to see any compensation. I will certainly not make this trip unless the amount has been clarified. So far, not a penny has been sent my way."

"I completely understand, my little one and I can say this, all of your expenses will be taken care of, and upon the completion of the tour, and a nice stipend will be awaiting you. Furthermore you will receive generous royalties from the sale of the book. For the grand finale, awaiting you at the airport is something you have wanted for a long time."

"Oh, damn! Don't tell me ... does it start with an A"

"You bet it does."

"An Avro Avian!" Amelia said with much excitement.

"Serviced and ready to go," G. P. replied, smiling from ear to ear.

This satisfied Amelia, although not a word was mentioned of the many extra-curricular activities she was expected to participate in. It made no never-mind to her. She had what was close to her heart, a plane of her own, but the title would stay in G. P.'s name.

After the tour, Amelia was provided with the comforts of G. P.'s stylish home in Rye, New York, as promised, where he was able to oversee the book she was to write on The Friendship trip across the Atlantic. She did have a good grasp of grammar, but was no match when compared to Putnam, the publisher, when it came to editing, formatting, and just the general readability of the prose. She was comfortable staying at his home and his wife, Dorothy, had become one of her best friends. Dorothy came from a wealthy family that had a claim to an element of fame in their own right. Her father, Edwin Binney, had been the creator of Crayola Crayons, which created a vast amount of wealth for the family. In 1931, Dorothy built a home in Fort Pierce Florida where her father had a winter home. She died in1982 after having lived a full life. It is notable that Amelia never visited her at this residence.

The only thing that gave Amelia any amount of concern was the realization GP was harboring feelings for her and she knew not whether it was love or just plain lust. For her part, she did not discourage his advances, because she did feel an admiration for the way he seemed to have a handle on her direction in life. At this point, she did not realize he was becoming a father figure to her. Eventually, this attraction would culminate in a low point in her future.

This small plane she received, the Avro Avian, was not noted for its reliability, but she fell in love with it and decided to fly it across the continent. The little biplane would cause many problems before she decided to sell it. On the very first day of her trip across the country, she landed in Pittsburgh, and while taxiing across Rogers Field, because of her innate carelessness, she ran into a ditch and caused more than incidental damage. The incident brought to the forefront an inborn trait; she would trivialize the accident and become angry when a reporter asked about it. She absolutely would not entertain anyone questioning her abilities. This characteristic followed her for the rest of her life and more than likely contributed to her eventual demise.

Continuing her adventure, she was forced down in Pecos, Texas where she made a forced landing on the main street of the city because of a valve problem in the engine, and again at Lovington, New Mexico. Later, when traversing the mountains, she allowed her engine to overheat and landed at a ranch in Douglas, Arizona. After repairs, she flew it to Yuma, and preparing to take off, she allowed an enthusiastic crowd to push the plane to a more desirable spot. In so doing, they toppled the plane, causing a bent propeller. Amelia, being self-sufficient, hammered the prop back into shape and away she went. She finished the trip without further incident at Glendale, California.

The next day, she arrived in Los Angeles to make an appearance at the National Air Exhibition show, an annual event. A crowd of thousands gave her a standing ovation and she and Lindbergh stole that show of shows.

On her Easterly return flight, more problems with the Avro took place. The motor quit one-hundred miles south of Salt Lake City and she had to make a dead stick landing. This time, the replacement parts took ten days to be delivered. While there, she had eager hosts who wanted her to make appearances and relate the various events that had taken place in her recent adventures. Amelia was more than happy to comply and her personality endeared her to everyone. She was the shining example of an American heroine.

Character flaws occasionally would show up, however. In Omaha, she found the airfield did not have the proper attendants and the plane had never been serviced. As if that were not enough, someone had folded the wings on her plane improperly. This was merely an irritation, but it left her in complete disbelief. More serious, souvenir hunters cut pieces of fabric from her plane, which was a horrendous breach of etiquette, but to add insult to injury, they returned to Amelia asking her to autograph the torn pieces! So taken back by such effrontery, anger emanated from her person and she uttered words that were seldom heard in that day. She later related this incident to a reporter and made the comment that, someday, an accident would occur because of such nonsense.

The journey ended in New York on October thirteenth, and forthwith, G. P. presented her with an itinerary of appearances designed to boost sales of her book, now entitled, ***Twenty Hours Forty Minutes: Our flight in the "Friendship."*** This schedule was of an ambitious nature to say the least, but pushing its sales was necessary because of its limited ability to hold the interest of many readers. The book held too many boring details.

The tour culminated in her being the featured speaker and personality at the twenty-fifth anniversary of the Wright

Brothers first flight at Kill Devil Hills, North Carolina. Her picture was taken on December 17th at the monument commemorating that first flight. She stood between Orville Wright and Senator Hiram Bingham, President of the National Aeronautics Association.

For the balance of 1928, she spent time enchanting her mother with exploits while making the round trip in her little Avian from New York to California and back again. She made speeches in thirty cities and gave more than two-hundred interviews. She now felt aviation could provide a living for her and had come to the realization that, without G. P., all of it might not have been possible.

Electra Vega

Rare Criticism

The year, 1929, saw Amelia continue on the path of acquiring more expertise in handling various types of airplanes. She unashamedly took lessons and was assured by the instructor she was a talented student. Building on her personal ambitions, she took and passed her commercial air transport license and many knowledgeable aviation professionals endorsed her proficiency, but there were others who were confident she was amateurish in her handling of airplanes, especially after she acquired a plane called the Electra Vega. Faster and more powerful than anything she had flown before, and with its 200-horsepower, Wright, Whirlwind engines, it was notorious for it's hard-to-handle ways. Many faulted Amelia for her over-the-top confidence in her abilities, one of these a woman of noted abilities, Elinor Smith. She learned to fly at the age of twelve and was holder of the woman's solo endurance record, on course to set a second record. She invited Amelia to accompany her on a flight, and the young pilot accepted. This occurred in Newcastle, Delaware, where Smith had gone for the trials of a new plane.

During the trials, she claimed that, as soon as Amelia took over the controls their calm big bird suddenly lurched out of control and she henceforth considered Amelia an incapable amateur. Their views also differed on the attributes of the Vega. Smith claimed the Vega had all the glide capabilities of a boulder falling off a mountain and that was after she bought one. While getting ready for a Trans-Atlantic flight, Elinor ground-looped the Electra and seriously damaged it at Garden City, Long Island only four months later. Yet, *Amelia purchased that same plane and set two world records with it.*

Amelia was kept busy doing all the things necessary to keep the money flowing in. That was all well and good, but other women fliers were garnering the headlines and book sales and the calls for her appearances were dropping off. Of course it, was a clarion call for George Putnam to schedule another exploit for his money ticket and she was more than willing to oblige.

On Ms. Earhart's birthday, July twenty-fourth, she became one of the participants in a woman's cross-country air race, which would precede the Cleveland Air Races. The all-male committee for this event declared the women's race would start in Omaha instead of Santa Monica, where it was originally scheduled to start, thereby enabling the ladies to avoid flying over the Rocky Mountains, because, if they insisted on starting in Santa Monica, they would have to be accompanied by a male

navigator. Amelia was so incensed at the committee's buffoonery, she fired off a letter of protest to the men running this affair and then gathered together members of the press and expressed her vituperation in no uncertain
terms. The committee eventually relented and the race was on from Santa Monica, with a total of twelve women fliers.

Will Rogers

Will Rodgers, in his comedic observations of the human condition, labeled the race with a moniker, "The Powder-Puff Derby," that would stick forevermore, thus earning Amelia's enmity in perpetuity. Yet, nothing lasts forever and that was true of her grievances with Will Rodgers when he later wrote in one of his newspaper columns that he gave his complete support to those trailblazing, brave ladies and had nothing but admiration for their efforts, castigating the organizers for their regrettable selection of airports they had to use. His exact words were, "making them stop in every buffalo wallow that has a chamber of commerce."

The race took a terrible toll on the contestants. One way or another, accidents and mishaps happened to all of the ladies, including one death that occurred when a contestant's engine overheated and the plane went down while flying over the mountains near Wellton, Arizona. One of the accidents involved Amelia, but, as was her wont, she refused to take any of the blame. She once again carelessly landed and ran into a pile of sand, nosing the plane over.

At Columbus, Ohio, their last stop before Cleveland, they encountered an unruly crowd of eighteen-thousand that mobbed the runway, getting in the way of taxiing planes. As soon as they could, the pilots jumped on the wings and attempted to reach out to the other arriving contestants. That was not enough; the crowd tore holes and punched pencils through the fabric.

Arriving in Cleveland was not the end of their travails. Every morning, they arose at four a. m., went to the field to supervise the repairs and reconditioning of their planes, and soon after, were hauled in to sign autographs and satisfy the whims of the sponsors of this air race. Amelia finished third in the Derby and won $850, which, even in 1929, was a pittance for what she had endured, but it did keep her name before the public and would enhance her value to George Putnam.

Amelia entered one of five pylon races for women and was disqualified for missing one of the pylons. Commenting on her lack of skill, the great, closed course racer, Edna Gardner Whyte, said, "Amelia never had the skill to be a racer, nor did she have the necessary competitive spirit." Another great speed racer, Mary Haizlip agreed. It does seem personalities that had a great sense of self-worth and ego make statements that are incongruous and by making these allegations are trying to enhance their eminence in their field of endeavor. Of course, making these statements often tended to backfire. In this instance, the one taking the fire went on to greater fame and went down in history as one of the greatest of American aviation heroines and never in her life did she utter a hyperbole that brought shame to another person. The people that defamed her are no longer remembered. Amelia is immortal.

Lindbergh's Luster Fades

Trans Continental Airlines, referred to as TAT, (Trans Air Transport) employed both Charles Lindbergh and Amelia Earhart, more as ambassadors for the business than anything else. Anne Lindbergh, Charles wife, was a sweet woman and felt very fond of Amelia. The compliment was returned by Amelia who, if the truth be known was not very fond of Charles.

Charles and Anne Lindbergh

While a houseguest of Jack Maddux, the owner of TAT, she observed Lindbergh's rather cruel practical jokes. At one point, she was truly disgusted when Lindbergh dripped water on his wife's silk dress. Anne Morrow Lindbergh in turn, wheeled around and threw a glass of buttermilk on him. On another occasion, little nine-year-old Jack Maddux Jr., in his pajamas, approached his hero, Charles, to wish him goodnight. Lindbergh asked him if he would like to earn a quarter. The boy said he would. Lindbergh took a sheet of paper, made a funnel and put the small end down the front of the boys pajamas, gave him a quarter and told him to hold it high, and with his eyes closed see if he could drop it down the funnel. The boy agreed, and while his eyes were closed, Lindbergh took a pitcher of ice water and poured it in the funnel. This caused quite a bit of discomfort and

Winners and Losers

pain to the child. Charles, the great man Lindbergh, found this hilarious.

In view of the recent events that were revealed according to newspaper reports from Germany, Lindberg was not the epitome of decorum. Aside from hobnobbing with Hitler, he did his share of consorting with the German lassies and fathered several children, according to claims made in 2013, bolstered with bona fide, DNA evidence. He was a supporter of Hitler in the 1930's after observing the great Air Force Germany was in the process of building. Much of this can be forgiven because he was a patriot as he proved when flying combat missions for the United States during World War ll.

1929, the year the world seemed to end and the beginning of the dreaded 1930s, was one where Amelia continued on her prosperous ways, established an ongoing annuity for her mother Amy, and continued to work for TCA as a representative of the Pennsylvania Railroad. Thanks to Mr. Putnam, she had ironclad contracts that guaranteed their participation in her exploits.

Dorothy Putnam

Amelia was no slacker. She wanted to fly and fly some more, establishing record upon record for woman's aviation. In early 1929, while Amelia was getting ready for another race, she received a call from her good friend, Dorothy Putnam. Dorothy knew that her husband and Amelia had been very close for quite some time. Whether or not they had been intimate, Dorothy had no way of knowing, but she suspected that there had been surreptitious meetings between the two of them, if only because they had been thrown together so many times in very close proximity. Each needed the other and many business deals were finalized while both of them were far from home. Human nature being what it is, it would be foolish to not believe that intimacy had not been initiated. Dorothy for her part, had been having at least one documented affair of her own, and now she was making a call that she dreaded to make.

The Other Woman

"Amelia, I am delighted to have finally caught up to you. I know you are preparing for another race, but if I waited to call when you are not busy, the wait might be quite extensive and what I have to tell you cannot wait."

"Dorothy I am so glad you called. I hope all is well with you." Amelia, realizing this call was a little unusual, replied a little apprehensively.

With a catch in her voice, Dorothy said, "Please do not think unkindly of me, but I have known for some time that G. P. and you have been very close, so I have today filed divorce papers. That means you and he now have at least one impediment removed toward your future happiness."

"Oh no, please, Dorothy! Never, *never* did I think that this would ever come to a place that I would be the catalyst causing unhappiness to another person, especially a good friend. I want you to know that I have no intention of getting married to anyone."

"Listen to me Amelia, you are not the reason this has happened. It has been fomenting for a considerable length of time. Believe me, you had nothing to do with what is occurring. All the fault lies with me. I no longer want a part-time marriage. I want someone who is there at night to have dinner with and enjoy moonlit walks, in other words, a real traditional union. I want the things that encompass love, if there is such a thing."

"Please Dorothy, let me express my heartfelt sorrow this has taken place. Is there anything that I can do to make amends? If there is, just let me know and I will go to the ends of the earth to repair any damage I may have caused."

"Amelia, your future is so bright; I have nothing but admiration for you. Just keep on doing what is making you a star and a living icon that everyone in this world can look up to, and every time I see your name in the paper and some new exploit that you have undertaken, I can say to myself I am just so proud to be your friend."

Finding herself to be the other woman in a marriage, caused Amelia to be disgusted with herself. The problem she was presented with became an either or situation. Either she continued a relationship with G. P. and received all of the benefits that accrued—namely a wealthy benefactor and personal energetic promoter who was the catalyst for the things she had become and the catalyst for further exploits commensurate with the fame that lays ahead—or, she would be left struggling to provide for a lifestyle that required mendacious amounts of capital. The first choice, however, would be at the cost of her friendship with Dorothy, her best friend.

G. P. could never be the romantic that a girl could dream of, but he would be the man that could make Amelia's dreams come true. But did she really know what those dreams were? At this stage of her life, probably not. There was a fire inside, driving her to continue flying and taking chances, doing things that nobody else before her had ever done. She did want to prove that women were the equal of men, but there was something else driving her, a gnawing inside that she could never quantify. What made her want to spend hour after hour in uncomfortable conditions squeezed into areas hardly big enough to accommodate even her slim figure? A woman was at a definite disadvantage when the call came to empty her bladder. This, of course, required her to wear diapers and caused much embarrassment when arriving at her destination. Yet, she considered these just small distractions to be endured.

It was not long after Dorothy's announcement of the divorce that Amelia and George were married on February seventh, 1931. This occurred with many misgivings on her part. He pursued her as fervently and insistently as other things he wanted, but Amelia made it known to him that this marriage would not be one involving a process where she would ever become the quintessential wife. In fact, she wrote him in a letter expressing her views.

I want you to understand I shall not hold you to any medieval code of faithfulness to me, nor shall I consider myself bound to you similarly.

The foregoing she adhered to rigorously for the rest of her incomplete life.

Conquer the Atlantic

Winners and Losers

1932 became the year that Amelia would finally do the thing that she had dreamed of ever since she made the crossing of the Atlantic in the Friendship as a passenger. Now, she would duplicate Lindbergh's feat. Several pilots made the crossing since Lindy and were successful, but they did not attempt the trip alone. Two had tried it solo and died. Four others, who tried with a partner, died. She wanted to do this exploit to prove to her doubters that she had the courage, proficiency, ability, and expertise to complete this hazardous journey.

Great secrecy was accorded to this venture. Her plane, the Electra Vega, the same one she had an accident with earlier, was registered to Bernt Balchen, a well-known aviator for Admiral Byrd, who had expertise in re-outfitting injured airplanes. He was also useful in maintaining the secrecy that Amelia required. Most folks thought that he was preparing for his next arctic trip. Balchen and an assistant flew many hours in the Vega using sandbags to determine the amount of fuel the plane was capable of carrying. It was established that a range of over 3,000 miles was its capability, more than enough for its proposed trip. Because of the treacherous Atlantic, instruments were added to enable Amelia to fly blind if necessary. She needed to go back to school with Balchen as the instructor to correct her deficiency in instrument flying.

On a beautiful spring day in April, showing a great amount of impatience, Amelia turned to Balchen while they were playing a game of croquet and asked with apprehension, "Am I ready?"

Balchen, without any hesitation, answered. "The plane is ready and so are you."

On May 20th, 1932, the fifth anniversary of Lindberg's historic trans-Atlantic flight, she lifted off from Harbor Grace, Newfoundland, seemingly without a care in the world. Not far into the flight, she encountered a severe thunderstorm and the fight was on, now she cared. To compound matters, her altimeter failed, and flying in the dark, she had no idea how high or low she was flying. When she put the Vega into a climb to get high enough to fly over the storm, the plane started picking up ice, which forced her back into the storm. Her manifold cracked and the engine was spewing flames from the exhausts.

Flying low enough not to ice up and high enough for her instruments to work, along with the cockpit filling up with fumes from the broken manifold, tested her skills to such an extent that an involuntary prayer was offered up. The gauge on one of her fuel tanks was broken and she no longer knew how much fuel was in the tank, which made Paris out of the question.

Reaching the northern coast of Ireland, she spotted a pasture filled with cows. She figured, to hell with the cows, and put the Vega down among the frightened cows and one frightened herder. To him, this was the strangest sight he had ever seen. He summoned his courage, he called out to her.

"Where are you from?"

"From America," she replied.

At this point, if she would have said Heaven, he would have immediately dropped to his knees and kissed her feet.

Amelia, the maestro of the three-ring circus and the master of the hunt, now ruled the air, the earth, and the sea, simply because she had just put on an unparalleled performance of courage and aviation skill no woman, and for that matter damned few men, had. Every accolade that came her way she deserved. She was no longer a young prodigy; she was now a grown-up wizard of the air. One of the few derisive comments she received came from London newspapers that had criticized her in the past, calling her "vain and foolish." Another saw it as a "magnificent display of useless courage." The negative comments, however, were few and muted. The tributes were many, and in the process, she even attracted the attention of the future king of England, who danced an inordinate number of dances with the attractive Amelia at a ballroom in London. Selfridge, the department store magnate, had her plane put on display in his department store.

Winners and Losers

∞∂∞

After a triumphant tour, she returned home. She needed time to herself away from the "Maddening crowds." Down, deep inside, she did not enjoy the unreasoning adulation that accompanied the pushing, screaming, grabbing multitudes. At times, she felt her life was in danger; at the very least, injuries were a distinct possibility. She felt safest when flying high and fast, trying to achieve a new record, either the longest, the fastest, or the highest, her fate in her own, two hands, gripping the controls of an airplane.

The Almighty had not been kind to Amelia; he forgot to attach the most important part of her anatomy… *wings*.

The Presidential Connection

The Bendix Air Race from Los Angeles to Cleveland was a race that Amelia fully intended to enter, especially since the director was very much chauvinistic, and in every way, would look for excuses to eliminate women from competing. She would become antagonistic to the director and decided to bring her considerable resources to bear if she had to. With her celebrity status came the ability to call on the highest office in the land for help if she had to. The White House and the Roosevelt's.

Eleanor Roosevelt felt a close connection with Amelia, since she felt they were so much alike and neither stood on pomp and circumstance. The first meeting took place soon after FDR was elected to office and Eleanor was none too happy with the role she would be required to play as the First Lady. Holding teas and entertaining visiting diplomats was not her idea of an exciting existence.

A half hour drive from Hyde Park, home of the Roosevelt's, Amelia was engaged at a local high school, giving an afternoon discourse on the subject, The Fun of Flying, along with motion pictures depicting events in Amelia's adventures.

Eleanor, along with a close friend, decided to attend this lecture. The First Lady walked into the auditorium, and as soon as she spotted Amelia, ran over and they spontaneously hugged each other.

"My God Mrs. Roosevelt," Amelia said. "I had no idea you were coming until the Secret Service showed up."

President Roosevelt and Eleanor

"Please, dear girl, call me anything you want, but not Mrs. Roosevelt. Listening to that all day long is rather tiring. I want you to know that I'm as excited as a little girl, getting to meet America's Sweetheart."

"Eleanor, I am but an ant compared to the giants of the world that you and Franklin have become."

Eleanor gave her a look of great significance. "You have no idea how much I want to be *you*."

After Amelia's presentation, which emphasized all of the things about women's equality with men that Eleanor wanted to hear, she launched into her soaring flights of derring-do, not only the grandeur of the successes, but also the deep, depressive moments when impending disaster loomed ahead.

Eleanor was so moved by her oration that she rushed up to Amelia after the speech, and with her high-pitched voice even higher, told her, "I want you to attend a dinner party at the White House this coming Friday. Bring whoever you want. Just tell me you will not disappoint us, because I know that Franklin is especially keen on meeting you."

"You can depend on it and I will be bringing George Putnam, who will be thrilled to be there."

From there on out, she was the one White House guest who had an open invitation to visit at her slightest whim.

The dinner engagement was a salutary expression of mutual respect, admiration, and trust. Roosevelt was known for his roving eye and had a well-developed sense of beauty. In this case, it was not the beauty but his sense Amelia had a quality in her personality that foretold greater adventures to come. He had an uncanny penchant discovering the hidden side of a person's abilities.

When observing Amelia, many people's first thought was, *she is pretty and has a compromising personality.* She was adept at keeping the fire and intensity that was her real temperament hidden, but both Franklin and Eleanor were pros when it came to discovering things in a person's character other people never would guess.

The dinner party was a success, with the Roosevelt's vastly entertained by the soaring rhetoric of George Putnam. Amelia, for her part was quiet while savoring the trappings and inwardly thrilled thinking of the history that had taken place in the exclusive home of Presidents. During dinner, Amelia broke the news she had arranged for a plane, standing by with pilot, to take Eleanor on a nighttime ride over Washington. Eleanor, of course, was thrilled, but did look askance at Franklin, who in turn assented with some amount of trepidation. Franklin would have liked to accompany his guests on this adventure, but the problem his wheel chair would have caused was not worth the trouble.

The participants trouped to the airport in their evening clothes, where a twin-engine Condor provided by Eastern Air Transport was waiting. Eleanor was thrilled when the pilot allowed her to take the controls for a while. Additionally, she had been offered the opportunity to get her pilot's license through Amelia, but Franklin nixed the idea. His excuse was that they did not have enough money to buy a plane. As laughable as that seems, there may have been some element of truth to it. Their home in Hyde Park did not belong to Roosevelt, it belonged to his family. The only piece of real estate that he owned was the small home in Warm Springs, Georgia. His personal estate may not have been as large as one would naturally believe.

From this point forward, Amelia would enjoy a warm relationship with both Franklin and Eleanor. It was true that the Roosevelt's marriage essentially had ended at an earlier time, since, in the past, Eleanor made the statement, that sex was something that had to be endured. Apparently, there was a vast disconnect there because they had six children. This rapport with the depression administration led to Franklin consulting with Amelia on anything concerning aviation, including highly-valued appointments to high office. Eleanor's inclination was to create more government agencies and exercise control over commerce. Liberalism seemed to be a part of her nature, yet her very independence and inherent toughness belied that aspect of her character.

∞∂∞

1933 and 1934 proved to be profitable years for Amelia although very tiring. She was a much sought after lecturer and highly-paid endorser of many products. It was at this time she started an Amelia Earhart line of fashion clothing. On top of that, she was offered a teaching position at Purdue University, instructing new students in choosing careers. All in all, this depression time of the thirties proved to be a time when, through no fault of her own, she lost contact with the suffering going on in America. Her world now embraced celebrities and others who occupied esteemed positions in government and business. Whenever asked to give of her time and money, she was always willing but, of course, airplanes remained dominant in her life and she longed to get back to flying.

Instinctively, she wanted to live on the West Coast. More than that, she wanted to be in a place where snow and cold were just a dim memory and beauty sat right outside your window. She left G.P. in New York and rented a home in North Hollywood, California. She still followed his instructions to some degree, but, with the passing years, she felt less and less in need of his direction. The attachment she had felt for him was turning into displeasure with the pushiness he displayed in promoting himself, and his interests, in a fashion that at times, made her cringe. When a photographer was taking pictures of Amelia, G. P. was sure to push his way into the photo and snickering among the reporters and the photographers behind his back was common.

In her mind the next adventure was forming, something no one else had done before, man or woman. She conceived this undertaking, a solo flight from Hawaii to California, a distance of over two thousand miles. In all previous ventures, Amelia tried and generally succeeded in keeping the trip a secret. She boarded a ship called the Lurline for Honolulu with her plane, the Lockheed Vega, lashed down on the fantail of the ship. No matter how many excuses she gave for the reason the plane was on the ship, the reporters were not put off; they knew that another colossal attempt of a new record would be made in some direction.

As the news sources became surer of their forecasts, negativity became rampant. The *Honolulu Star-Bulletin* wrote: "If Amelia Earhart intends to fly solo from Hawaii to the mainland, then some authority ought to stop her. A transpacific flight in a single engine plane is idiotic. Everything we need to know about flying to the mainland is already known. If she fails, the ghastly search will begin with the taxpayers footing the bill." The Army, in the person of Lieutenant Leroy Hudson, sent an inquiry to the Bureau of Air Commerce asking if there were any restrictions on the type of equipment required on transpacific flights of a single-engine airplane. The Bureau wired back that there were no limitations. The *Star-Bulletin* followed up with: "Although no laws were infringed, it is our concern for the safety of Amelia," and they offered up platitudes for her courage and gumption.

John Williams, a reporter, kept hammering away on the subject. Why, he wanted to know, did the Army allow her freely to use the Army's base for maintenance and installation of various devices that were unknown to the general public? He charged that they had installed a telegraph unit Amelia did not know how to use. Other questions of such nature were raised. Who paid for the four-hundred-fifty gallons of fuel the plane was topped off with? Why was the plane outfitted with photographic equipment, all at the expense of the taxpayers? Why was there a need for this hush-hush equipment?"

Events intervened to delay this excursion.

War Fever

Prior to this excursion, and before she went to the West Coast, Amelia received an important communication from Franklin Roosevelt through a courier. The message was addressed, *For Your Eyes Only*, requesting her immediate presence at the White House, ostensibly for a luncheon, but the message was more of a command than a request. The tone of it indicated there was urgency about it.

Amelia was escorted to the executive living quarters, where few visitors ever had the privilege of going. She met the President and the First Lady in the sitting room and was a little unsettled at the seriousness of their expressions. As usual, Eleanor expressed her delight at once again seeing Amelia, but Franklin had a rather dour look about him. Whenever he spoke, he usually had an energizing smile and an easy casual manner. However, this afternoon, his mood was serious and his voice took on an oratorical tone.

"My dear, what you will hear today must, and will, carry great significance to America. Everything that is here discussed will never be disclosed outside of this room. In you, I have placed a major amount of trust in your ability to carry the confidential matters of this meeting to your grave, if necessary. No one outside of this room and essential governmental staff can give voice to anything heard here. Can I be assured of your confidentiality?"

The tone of Amelia's voice was fervent in her ardent response. "Mr. President, I have the highest regard and trust in you and will absolutely adhere to a sealed lips policy."

"Before we get to business, I suggest we have an afternoon brandy and lunch." Franklin said.

Amelia spoke about her disapproval of alcohol, citing the fact that, in her business, a clear head was essential. She did confess that a healthy appetite was eternal in her case. She did not find it necessary at the time to reveal that her father was an alcoholic.

"I suppose that in my business a clear head is also essential, but the hell with that. What I propose to talk about today is something that may require two brandies," Franklin declared.

Lunch was a stilted affair. Franklin and Eleanor seemed to be deep in thought and neither seemed to have much interest in their food. The same could not be said for Amelia. Her ravenous appetite was in full bloom, even though the atmosphere was not as conducive to enlightened conversation as in the past.

Suddenly, Eleanor stood up. "My dear girl, as much as I would like to have a pleasant conversation with you, I must take my leave. What you and Franklin have to discuss has world implications and both of you need to have space to deliberate this matter. I do want to get together with you when we will have more time to consider the more pleasant aspects of our lives. You tend to be secretive when it comes to plans you may be making, but, whatever your strategies are I'm sure they will be earth shaking."

"My plans are still in the formative stage, but whatever happens, upon my return I will be able to regale you with feats of derring-do," Amelia said, laughing and went on to say, "I have every intention that I will return in triumph."

Her lighthearted manner finally brought a smile to FDR's face, since his natural inclination was to maintain a sunny disposition, but he became serious again. "They call you the Queen of the Sky, but whoever termed that phrase forgot to add heaven. I think that the appropriate terminology would be Queen of the Heavens. Possibly I can use that when we assign you a code name."

"Why in the world would I need a code name?"

"Because, young lady, I am going to ask you to do something ... not for me, not for yourself, not for aviation, but for your *country*."

"Mister President, anything that my country asks of me I will do if I am capable of completing the mission. I know that you hold a high estimation of my abilities, but you may find me unqualified to carry out expectations above my proficiencies."

The President, with just a touch of impatience, responded. "Amelia, *please*, I have a modicum of intelligence. I have followed your exploits with a great deal of interest, and in my estimation, your achievements were monumental in what you were trying to do for the women of this world and the expertise you personally exhibited."

"Mr. President, I did not mean to cast aspersions on your intelligence. I just meant to convey that I may not have the attributes you think I have. I know in the future, the American public will hold you in the highest regard. I'm merely hopeful, in the years to come, that someone will remember my name with a measure of respect."

The President sighed. "Japan has been preparing for war for many years. Their aim is to control all of Asia. In order to accomplish that mission, they must sterilize and make America impotent. They have already engaged the British and the strength of the British Empire in the Pacific is minimal at this time. They hold a great animosity to the United States, primarily because of our policy of denying them their lifeblood, which is oil. At some point, they will attack us. I do not know where or how, but they will."

A shocked Amelia responded. "My God, Mister President, what you are telling me is that we may be on the brink of war!"

Nodding, Franklin went on. "It may not happen today, or tomorrow, but I am certainly of the opinion that, at this very moment, they are preparing a confrontation with the United States."

"And what role do you think I could play in this terrible possibility?" Amelia asked.

"This is exactly why you are here today. We need intelligence, the kind that will tell us where the Japanese are building fortifications. There are literally thousands of islands in the Pacific. Any one of them could be a jumping-off spot for an invasion of the U. S. mainland, or any one of our possessions. The mission I have for you is to scout out and photograph the locations that could be a threat to the United States."

"Oh for heaven's sake, Franklin, you are asking me to be a spy. This goes against everything that I have ever believed in.

You know that I have been a pacifist all my life, and now you want me to help my country prepare for *war*."

"Yes Amelia, "I want you to help me keep the country that has nurtured us and gave us the right to live in freedom, a country that was born with the express purpose to give all people the right to live in freedom. Yes, that is what I am asking you to do."

With trepidation, Amelia replied. "Mr. President, you will have my complete cooperation in this endeavor. Now, her practical side made its appearance, "let's get down to the implementation of this plan."

"I can tell you this," Franklin went on. "I know about your plan to fly solo from Hawaii to California. I am not at liberty to tell you how we obtained this information, but be advised that the secrecy of your expedition has been compromised. One of the first areas we will explore is the tightening of the secrecy surrounding your planned operations. In order to expedite this, I will have one of our FBI operatives get in touch with you. Starting now, all expenses for your activities will be provided by the government and will be done in a covert manner that includes your choice of an airplane. The funding of the plane will come through Purdue University, which currently has you on their staff."

"I am thoroughly appalled that the object of my trip has been compromised," Amelia replied.

"I am sad to tell you, this is the last time you will visit with Eleanor or me until the expedition has been completed."

Amelia, with an undercurrent of apprehension, responded. "Have you already decided what options are currently in the works?"

"Yes we have, but many of the decisions will be left up to you, with the final approval decided by my very competent staff, of course."

The meeting finally drew to a close and saw the very tired Aviatrix stagger to her room, her head in a whirl. That morning, the only thing on her mind was the next record she would try to set. Now, at the end of the day, she had become a spy for the United States Government. Her life was now topsy-turvy. She could usually sleep through a hurricane, but, on this night, sleep would not come.

Hawaii, the Trial Run

That one reporter had Amelia worried and a contact from the FBI was with her everywhere she went. Nevertheless, conferring with him and letting him shoulder some of the burden, gave her a measure of mental relief. The advice that was offered was simple in its affectedness: Amelia should go about her plans, ignoring all criticisms without responding. Using that approach took the sting and fire away from reporters, or others seeking celebrity status through controversy.

She wrote Major Clarke at Wheeler Field a note to be delivered in the event of her demise. *If the test take-off proves satisfactory, I plan to try for the mainland. It is clearly understood that the Army is in no way chargeable with any responsibility connected with the flight. You did for me only what you would do for any other responsible pilot, properly pointing out the risks involved. I assume the entire responsibility for the flight.*

Friday, January eleventh, the scheduled flight would leave Wheeler Field and wing towards the mainland. That event finally happened at 4:30 p. m. The newspapers were filled with the trial of Bruno Hauptmann in the kidnapping of the Lindberg baby. This event worked to the benefit of this trial flight, taking the spotlight from Amelia and blunting any more speculation and criticism aimed at her. The Government in no way wanted to alert the Japanese of this flight that might be flying over territory that had significance to Japan.

Amelia's courage was remarkable, faced with an airfield that was substantially mud, her plane loaded with a great deal of fuel and one she did not have overwhelming confidence in. On top of that she had to be thinking of the role she would be playing in world events. She wrestled with her mental state, knowing that whatever happened, would have consequences for the entire world. Apprehension became a way of life for her.

Winners and Losers

The flight proved eventful. Fog was heavy, she could not receive radio frequencies vital to her positioning, a ventilation cover blew off the fuselage, resulting in air streaming into one of her eyes, causing it to swell and almost close. If it had not been for the significance of this test flight, she almost certainly would have turned back or aborted the expedition at the beginning.

At 1:30 p. m. the next day, she landed in Oakland. Thousands of admirers crowded the field and she was absolutely mobbed and jostled; admirers and reporters exhibiting their usual lack of manners and not having the slightest bit of empathy for her condition, continuing to pummel her with questions while she swayed on her feet, too tired to give a cogent answer.

FDR and Eleanor wired congratulations, breaking with his past declaration of no contact with her in the future. This was done with an eye toward allaying possible speculation that the Government had anything to do with Amelia's activities. Thus, he invited Amelia to the White House.

∞∂∞

This latest success also caused George Putnam a great amount of joy and sent him into a state of euphoria. The intoxicating scent of copious amounts of money made him redouble his efforts to arrange personal appearances, speeches, interviews, and endorsements for Amelia and the schedule he presented to her was impossible to fulfill. She pushed back in her inimitable way, ignoring some of it, apologizing for some of it, and making excuses for the rest of it. Amelia did have an appreciation of money so she did extend herself to do what she could.

With the promised backing of the Government, she did not have the pressure to acquire enormous amounts of funding. The secret she promised to keep was, to her, sacrosanct, not to be revealed, even to her husband. It was a secret she carried to her watery grave.

Flying from Burbank, Ca. to Mexico City, thence non-stop to Newark, NJ, was the next performance of The Amelia Earhart Show, produced by the inimitable maestro, George Putnam. William Lear, the inventor of a radio homing compass, announced it would be installed on her plane. As a result of testing this device. FDR's Air Commerce Director, Gene Vidal, who owed his appointment to Amelia, named her as one of FDR's dollar-a-year experts.

As a result of poor weather, she changed her flight plans and lost her way, resulting in an unplanned landing on a lakebed in Nopala, sixty miles from Mexico City and 100 miles off course. A gaggle of the local vaqueros pointed her in the right direction and she soon arrived at her destination amid a cacophony of thousands of people.

On the morning of May 8th, she lifted off in a plane heavily loaded with fuel Using a route suggested by the great aviator, Wiley Post. She had originally wanted to fly over the Gulf of Mexico until she consulted with him. He pointed out that it was too dangerous and she, thinking highly of his skills, immediately changed her plans. Ironically, Post was killed, along with Will Rogers, on August 15, 1935, three months after advising Amelia of the safest route to take. His supreme confidence in his abilities led him to installing improper pontoons on his aircraft, safety and common sense be damned, and that led to their demise.

As expected, Amelia set another new record and was properly feted, causing her celebrity status to increase to unimaginable heights. Now, the praise increased for Amelia exponentially and decreased for G. P. into the gutter, where most critics believed he belonged. She did not seem to care what the news of the day said about him, and as she did with most criticism, she used her innate charm to ignore it.

The Final Adventure

In consultation with the Government, by the end of 1935 and the beginning of 1936, her ultimate plan started to take shape. She informed G. P. that she wanted to make an around the world trip solo, the first by a woman. G. P. almost fell over with excitement. The amount of income this would generate would be enormous and thinking about it sent him into spasms of effort. His concern seemed to be with the amount of capital this venture would bring in and he cared not a fig about Amelia's safety.

The more she got into the planning, the more she realized the hundreds of details that had to be considered. The number one thing on her list of priorities was a new airplane. She already knew what she wanted, but G. P. insisted that he be the go-between of the various manufacturers, trying to win concessions on price. He brought in Paul Mantz, a very close friend of his and a well-respected person in the field of aeronautics, desiring his expertise in this area. G. P. ignored the fact that Paul's wife was suing him in a bitter divorce suit, claiming Amelia as the responsible party, having had intimate relations with her husband. Whether true or not, G. P. did not seem to care. It is true that Amelia had spent some time at The Mantz's home, while his wife was elsewhere, which Paul denied.

Allowing GP to take the lead in the organization of this event, was Amelia's way of dodging any confrontations, knowing that, in the end, she would be the final arbiter. Paul Mantz was aware of this fact and gave G. P. his due, but was always in contact with Amelia on any acquisitions or additions to be made to her aircraft. Amelia, in turn, was in contact with the Government agent, informing him on plans that were being formulated. Unbeknownst to her, he was providing security protection as much as possible, while she exposed herself to multitudes of people. Not only was she taking risks in her flying profession, but greater risks took place when she would be appearing before thousands of spectators and mingling with them.

Amelia needed permits to fly over foreign territory and was badly in need of the help from the U. S. Navy. In both cases, she had trouble getting the proper responses. After waiting two months for the Navy to provide an answer to her requests, she fired off letters to both Eleanor and Franklin. The answers she wanted came back from the department handling permit paperwork and the Navy, forthwith, with apologies and assurances that all matters would be expedited.

Howland Island, a little spritz of dirt under the administration of the United States, was selected, ostensibly by G. P., but decided on by the Government. The administration was aware of the Japanese expansion plans in Asia and felt that an airbase and supply depot there may come in handy at this particular spot. This avoided the allegation that it was built with only Amelia Earhart in mind. There had already been finger-pointing on her previous trips of the Government wasting taxpayer money on a private, ego trip.

Amelia's mother in-law, Francis Putnam, passed away during the time she was staying with Amelia. George Putnam was not there at his mother's death, but he arrived soon after when Amelia expressed concern that his mother was near death. This was not a good sign for Amelia and she took it hard. In the profession that she had chosen, she was not a stranger to death, but not this close to her.

Within weeks, she accepted delivery of her new Electra, with powerful, twin, 550 horsepower Wasp engines. She immediately started taking familiarity lessons from two experienced pilots, Paul Mantz and Elmer McLeod. She had a difficult time becoming proficient at handling this giant of a plane, but she was thrilled with its flight characteristics, speed, responsiveness, and pure power. It was the same feeling that became evident when handling a great racehorse.

Mantz was not at all satisfied with her handling of this flying machine and he continually urged her to spend more time flying the elegant-but-cantankerous marvel. She had many commitments to keep, and with her financial arrangements, there was no way she would not keep all her obligations.

With consultations between her and Mantz, it was decided she would enter the 1936 Bendix National Air Race, to begin at the Floyd Bennett Field in New York and head to Los Angeles. This would allow more time to become accustomed to the new Electra 10e. With Mantz and her mechanic, Bo McNeeley, she departed Burbank. Their first stop would be Kansas City and then on to New York.

Amelia had taken possession of the Electra on her birthday, July 24th, 1936. She was 39 years old, but, like a kid at Christmas, she could hardly contain how thrilled she was with the aircraft. To add to her glee, she paid nary a sou for the new possession, titled in her name, complements of the United States Government through Purdue University.

Only seven planes were entered in the race and three were women, much to the chagrin of the officials of the race, who still harbored anti-woman sentiments. The number of ladies entered delighted Amelia. She originally told reporters she would fly solo, but eventually decided to take her good friend, Helen Richey, as her co-pilot. So, in the dark of the night they started the race, on September 4th, 1936.

Not long after lift-off, it was lucky for Amelia that Helen was along. The hatch lock gave way and Helen had to hold it down until Amelia was able to get the plane in autopilot mode. It took both of them to secure the cover. Various problems occurred during the race, which contributed to Helen and Amelia finishing in fifth place. The good news to Amelia was the fact that two women flying together finished a harrowing race. The upside to her? She was able to spend a considerable amount of time gaining experience with her new aircraft.

By August, the Commerce Department granted her a license for her planned around the world flight, restricted to long distance flights and research. The research part of it gave something for many people to ponder. What exactly was the research that would occur on the flight?

∞∂∞

An Affair Remembered

Gene Vidal and Amelia

By this time, Amelia's marriage to George Putnam was, for all practical purposes over, and her intentions were now centered on one Gene Vidal. This was evident in the many times they were together. She went on to use her influence to get Gene his appointment reconfirmed by FDR as Director of Air Commerce. When FDR was reorganizing that department, one of the positions to be eliminated was that held by Gene. Amelia, who was an ardent FDR supporter, threatened to quit his campaign, and in support of her position, sent a scathing letter to Eleanor, who in turn showed it to the President. FDR, who was very astute in affairs of the heart, felt this was the best laugh he had in a long time. Needless to say, Vidal retained his position.

Vidal had a tremendous admiration and respect for Amelia, but, in his mind, that was probably as far as the relationship went. She, on the other hand, was head over heels in love with this handsome man, spending as much time with him as her schedule would allow, and more than likely, brief sexual encounters ensued. He was everything that G. P. was not, notable among them, good manners and a deep, caring friendship. Plus, he had no interest in promoting her, or her fame.

Meeting Gene and attending a football game with him was heaven for Amelia. On a bright crisp November day together, they attended the Army-Navy game in Philadelphia. Gene, who had previously played football for the University of South Dakota and had taught aeronautics there, as well as serving as football quarterback coach at West Point, had a great interest in this game. Amelia, wanting to please Gene as much as possible, tried to learn as much as she could about football.

Gene recently divorced, but an excellent father, took his ten-year-old son, to the game. The younger Vidal and Amelia hit it off admirably, talking more about airplanes than about football. She asked him what his favorite thing was. Surprisingly, his answer was writing stories and he would become, in adulthood, the noted and very controversial writer, Gore Vidal.

After the game Gene, Amelia, and Gore returned to the hotel. They put the young man to bed and then retired to the lounge for a cocktail. For once, Amelia decided to have a libation and her attitude the entire evening was one of compliance, trying very hard to please Gene. Yet, she did not feel she had succeeded.

"Gene, I hope you were not too upset with the outcome of the game. I feel that Army was the superior team and was denied a victory by the wrong-headed call of one referee." (Navy upset Army, seven to nothing, after a very controversial call late in the game which went Navy's way.)

Gene looked at Amelia in a wan, distant way. "I guess, in life, we have to accept those things we cannot change."

"I do believe that is true, but we must try. Certainly you cannot change things that have happened in the past, however you can make damned sure those past mistakes are not repeated. Tell me Gene, do you and I have a chance or will this forever remain a one way romance?"

"Please forgive me Amelia; I know that I owe you so much, and I can never repay what you have done for me, but I must think of the future and what it holds for both of us. My life will be filled with sedate jobs that will be interesting to me. I will probably remain in one place as far as my living arrangements are concerned. I see it as a very blasé existence, when you, on the other hand, live in a world that is so far and above anyone's imagination it would make any person in your life seem dull."

"Never in my life have I ever been so in love with anyone as I am with you," Amelia responded. "I would gladly give up my situation and spend the rest of my life pleasing you."

"Ah, dear lady, you know not what you say. If we married, in six months you would be bored and wondering what the hell you'd done and start looking for the next adventure … without me."

Amelia spent the rest of the evening smarting over the tepid rejection she had received. Somewhere, down deep inside, she knew he was right, but, at this moment, all she wanted was his arms around her, expressing an enduring love. Amelia could be impetuous, displaying this characteristic when she decided to take on thrilling attempts at new exploits that were fraught with danger. She never gave a fig over what it could entail in the way of personal risk. This attitude was apparent in her feeling toward Vidal. He, on the other hand, was trained to be much more judicious in making his way in the world, thinking things through and then projecting them into the future before making a decision. Going it alone was natural for her, but, in some way, after the rebuff from Gene, she felt more alone than ever. Yet, the greatest achievement of her career—an around the world flight that was just a few months in the future—was beckoning and was still secret, except for those that needed to know.

∞∂∞

The planning for the around the world flight was well under way at the beginning of 1937. The plan, as it was originally formulated, was going from east to west, starting in California and ending on the east coast of the United States. The amount of things that had to be done was staggering. Permission had to be obtained from every country she would fly over, mid-air refueling had to take place with the un-willing cooperation of the Navy and fueling depots were to be established on intermittent islands across the Pacific. An airbase was constructed on tiny Howland Island, accomplished with the help of the Works Progress Administration (WPA), one of the cornerstones of the Roosevelt Administration's New Deal program.. A million other things of great importance had to be carried out, not to mention the entire load of overwhelming minutia that something of this magnitude required. All of this had to be carried out with maximum secrecy. Of course, this was not entirely possible, considering the number of countries that were involved.

FDR and Eleanor were asked to run interference on numerous occasions, where obstreperous officials, who were never informed that this flight was not just an ego trip of Amelia's, but a cooperative venture between her and the United States Government. Roosevelt was positive that the Japanese would strike one of our possessions in the Pacific, but he did not know where, or how. He hoped this voyage of Amelia's would gather sorely needed intelligence vital to the security of the nation. Consequently, he complied with anything that her consortium asked of his administration.

One of the most important decisions Amelia had to make was the choice of a navigator. Consulting with other knowledgeable personalities, using her past experience, brought up several, who, on the surface were qualified names. Finally, the names were reduced to only one, Fred Noonan, who seemed to have the experience required for such a mission. The only flaw that marred his capability was that he had been fired from a previous position because of his affinity for strong spirits. This was a recurring theme in Amelia's selections in the past, and this time, it may have contributed to her demise.

During late 1936 and early 1937, Amelia worked intensely with Paul Mantz and others. Each had a field of expertise that she would need. Pan American provided the radio direction finder that they had successfully pioneered on their "Clipper" ships over the Pacific. This was a new device of great importance and simplicity that would enable her to pinpoint her location with simple radio frequencies.

Test pilots, who had checked her out in the various areas of proficiency required, were generally laudatory toward her abilities. The one exception was Paul Mantz, who felt that she did not have the necessary nuances required in handling a powerful, twin engine aircraft. He never expressed his innate observation that women were lacking in the skill sets required to connect mentally with formidable, inanimate objects. His assessment proved correct, when, at the start of her sojourn from Hawaii, when taking off, she over-jockeyed the engines, causing the plane to ground loop, doing extensive damage to the plane. Enough damage occurred that the plane had to be dismantled and shipped back to the states for rebuilding. Amelia never accepted blame for the accident, but shifted the responsibility to a blown tire, yet seemed unsure of which tire it was. She also stated there may have been an imperfection in the runway. Whatever it was, Paul was sure it was pilot error.

Even though he was her friend, in the end he did cast criticisms on her abilities. He always thought that she should never have attempted this particular flight. He rightfully felt that she was taking undue risks in her chosen route, in particular the choice of Howland Island. It was a tiny speck of land in a vast ocean. Everything in his nature rebelled at the thought that he was about to lose a friend. This came about because of her uncompromising confidence in herself. His clairvoyance in this instance proved to be on the nose.

Winners and Losers

Another person who was close to Amelia, a best friend and well-known aviatrix in her own right, Jackie Cochran, had a premonition about this particular excursion Amelia was about to embark on. She was outspoken and loud in her negative views of G. P. and his choice of navigators. She felt that he was a money-grubbing bastard, who put money ahead of safety and the only reason Noonan was selected and pushed on Amelia was because of his inability to find a position, having been dismissed from his last position because of drunkenness. No other airline would hire him, so, consequently, he was willing to work below the standard rate. This was duly noted by the penny-pinching G. P. and was a factor in his selection of Noonan.

Amelia and Fred Noonan

Gene Vidal was also concerned about Amelia and he expressed his apprehensive feelings in notes between him and her, certain she was through with G. P. and his overbearing ways. Amelia always felt a thrill whenever she received a communication from Gene and her emotions ran so deep when thinking about him that she shared a secret with him, she considered him a good luck charm, and on every flight, she wore a pair of his jockey shorts.

∞∂∞

The Electra was ready on May nineteenth. A crew, assembled by Lockheed, worked overtime to get the plane assembled and ready for the around-the-world trip. Paul Mantz heard that Amelia had flown the plane to Oakland and was now ready to start her adventure from east to west, following a hastily made change of plans, ostensibly because of a change in worldwide weather patterns. Amelia had a healthy respect for bad luck and good luck omens, and after her experiences in Hawaii, she had decided that the better part of valor would be to ignore that island as a starting point, and instead, make it the next to last stop before completing the journey.

Paul Mantz

Mantz was not comfortable with this change of plans and his judgment, as usual, was impeccable, his reasoning being that this placed tiny Howland Island as her last stop before Hawaii, when she certainly would be tired and not in full control of her faculties, trying to find a tiny speck of land with a navigator who was an avowed alcoholic, plus her unfamiliarity with the radio equipment available to her. One apparatus that Amelia was loathe to use was a backup system for the five-hundred-frequency on her direction finder, making it possible for a ground station to receive an emergency SOS and get a fix on her location. To comply with this directive required her to unreel two-hundred-fifty feet of antenna while she was in the air and reel it back in when landing. Paul remembered how she had complained on a previous flight about this piece of equipment. Knowing Amelia, he was sure she would not install this device.

Amelia flew from Oakland to Tucson to New Orleans, encountering many imperfections in her plane. Finally, she arrived in Miami where the start of the trip would begin. She made an uncharacteristic hard landing and was a little embarrassed by it. At this point, she found herself having many apprehensions. An enlightening conversation she had with her friend, Jackie Cochran, revealed her state of mind. She gave Jackie a small, silk scarf as a memento.

"I would rather you keep this scarf, and when you get back, autograph it for me," Jackie said to Amelia.

"No I want you to take it now," Amelia replied.

She also related to another acquaintance, Carl Allen, "I have a feeling I will never return from this trip, but I have always had an abhorrence of growing old, so I won't feel completely cheated if I fail to come back."

The Final Adventure Ends

The Electra 10e, lost at Sea in 1937

At 5:56, on the morning of June 1st, 1937, with five-hundred spectators watching, Amelia lifted off from Miami on what would prove to be her last hurrah, the final journey of a life too short, too stormy and too fast paced. With no time for a real love—and too many people vying for what little time she had to give—what time she had, she gave willingly.

The complete route included thirty-three stops, which did not include unscheduled flyovers that the Government asked her to make in secrecy. The total number of miles would be; 28,595; approximately 24,285 actual miles.

The problems that occurred were unimaginable, including storms of every possible magnitude, from imminent hurricanes to tornados, flying blind, flying sick and vomiting while airborne, losing a significant amount of weight due to such sicknesses, having no idea of what the malady was. Noonan proved to be an excellent navigator; however, according to communications received from her, it was apparent she was struggling to keep him sober. Generally the plane performed admirably, all that she could have hoped for. The same could not be said for the radio equipment.

Her flight would be from Lae, Papau New Guinea, to Howland Island, a distance of twenty-five-hundred miles. Flying that distance to a small speck in the ocean was a test for Noonan, assuming he had a clear mind. The other aspects of an improperly working radio, combined with Noonan's and Amelia's incompetence with Morse Code, made that leg of the journey challenging, to say the least.

The Japan Connection

Where did Japan fit in to this global flight? Japan closely followed the planning of Amelia's planned exploit and knew two things. One, her route would take her over territory, or close to territory, that was highly critical to the planning of an engagement with the United States. Two, Amelia was a close friend of FDR and Eleanor. That was enough to prompt Japan to make her attempt a sterile endeavor.

Japan was in the throes of planning a war with the United States. The causes were primarily, at that time, an embargo by the United States of steel and oil, without which the Imperial Empire of Japan would not continue to exist. Japan knew, when

Winners and Losers

this embargo went into effect, there would be no alternative to war.

In 1937, Japan was already engaged in China and America's naval might was of serious concern to them. It was only a matter of time before she would launch a sneak attack on the United States, and hopefully, in one fell swoop with a well-planned assault, cripple America's ability to conduct warfare in the Pacific. In order to carry this out, they needed armed bases able to supply and resupply ships, men, and airplanes. Secrecy was of the utmost importance. By scattering their ordinance and supply depots on a wide variety of islands, they accomplished two things; the ability to avoid a concentrated attack and allocating resources with shrewdness that would support a covert attack on the "sleeping giant," in whatever form that might take.

∞∂∞

There were several ships deployed by the U.S. Navy in the area of Howland Island to intercept and send messages to Amelia when and if she was heard from. One ship, the *Itasca* laid down heavy smoke from her stacks to enable her and Noonan to home in on the location. The ship and the island radio operators were able to receive transmissions from Amelia's Electra, but most were either garbled or indistinct. However, a few came in clearly, but, apparently, Amelia did not hear their responses. This was due to the absence of the trailing radio antennae Amelia foolishly decided not to install, or a faulty fuse on her radio equipment, which had given trouble in the recent past and she did not give enough consideration of the need to trace the reason the fuse blew. She felt that replacing the fuse was all that was needed.

The last radio transmission from Amelia gave a heading of 157-dash-337 indicating they were running on a north/south line. More than likely, they had missed badly Howland Island, their calculations on the amount of fuel they had consumed inaccurate, and at the time they were running north and south, and were probably not as yet east of Howland. If they had been east of the Island, it would have been virtually impossible not to have seen the Itasca. They were probably on a north/south route, well *west* of the Island. Going north or south on the westerly side would have brought them into contact with Japanese ships, which were actively searching for the Electra.

This is only conjecture, but Japan was well aware of her activities and certainly would have been apprehensive and suspicious of the reason that Amelia was making the well-funded flight by the United States Government around the world, over territory, that was highly sensitive to Imperial Japan. Nothing would have pleased them more than to have blown that Electra from the sky, never to be found again. If that, indeed, happened, then the Electra and its occupants will never be found.

They lay at the bottom of the ocean in small pieces.

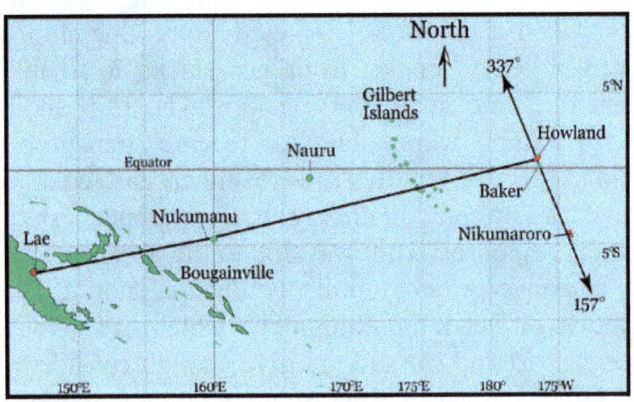

Recently a small piece of aluminum was found on Nikumaroro Island. Some feel it may have been a piece of Amelia's plane. Just another find that keeps the searchers well-funded with donations.

Amelia's Legacy

Amelia had many faults, but, then, who among us meets the requirements for perfection? I dare say, without a scant chance of being challenged, Amelia was not the best aviatrix that ever lived, nor was she the greatest adventurer who ever lived. She was also not the greatest scholar, nor the greatest daredevil, but, wherever men and woman look to the sky and dream of exploits yet to come, her name will be written in the book of knowledge and in the annals of past and future history.
    Forever.

Vaudeville
The introduction to Eva Tangquay

CHARLES E. GRAPEWIN

Did vaudeville exist? Not according to a recent survey I personally have undertaken of those sixty years old and under. This was difficult for me to comprehend, considering that form of show business was an integral part of the history of America.

The name, probably French in origin, first appeared at a theater in New York City. The concept was not original. It was a conglomeration of various acts put together in one show.

Prior to vaudeville, the terminology for these vestigial art forms were Minstrel Shows, performed many times in blackface, popular prior to 1860. The western part of the country entertained shows that were understandably more risqué in nature. Women were in high demand because of a dearth of the fairer sex and the dance halls of the Old West were populated with ladies of loose morals who doubled as dancers and strippers and were used in a venue referred to as burlesque and other sobriquettes as you can imagine, the audience being composed of rough hewn men; i. e. miners, cowboys, itinerant merchants, gamblers, and others of this ilk.

In the East, the shows were much more genteel in nature. A typical vaudeville performance was made up of a series of separate, unrelated acts, grouped together on a common bill. Types of acts included popular and classical musicians, singers, dancers, comedians, trained animals, magicians, female and male impersonators, acrobats, illustrated songs, jugglers, one-act plays or scenes from plays, athletes, lecturing celebrities, minstrel acts, and movies. A vaudeville performer was often referred to as a vaudevillian.

The date usually given as the birth of vaudeville was October 24, 1881, at a variety show at New York's 14th Street Theatre. By the late 1890s, vaudeville had large circuits and houses (small and large) in almost every sizable location, standardized booking, broad pools of skilled acts, and a loyal national following. One of the biggest circuits was B. F. Keith and the Albee Theatre' and Martin Beck's Orpheum Circuit. It brought together forty-five vaudeville theaters in thirty-six cities throughout the US and Canada and a large interest in two vaudeville circuits. Another major circuit was that of Alexander

Pantages. In his hey-day, Pantages owned more than thirty vaudeville theaters and controlled, through management contracts, perhaps sixty more in both the US and Canada. At its height, vaudeville played across multiple strata of economic class and auditorium size. On the vaudeville circuit, it was said that, if an act would succeed in Peoria, Illinois, it would work anywhere. The question "Will it play in Peoria?" has now become a metaphor for whether something would appeal to the American mainstream public.

The capitol of the "big time" was New York City's Palace Theatre, or just "The Palace" in the slang of vaudevillians. The theatre was built by Martin Beck in 1913, and operated by B F. Keith. Featuring a bill stocked with inventive novelty acts, national celebrities, and acknowledged masters of vaudeville performance, such as comedian and trick roper Will Rogers, the Palace provided what many vaudevillians considered the apotheosis of a remarkable career.

A standard show bill would begin with a sketch, followed with a single—an individual male or female performer—next would be an alley oop—an acrobatic act—then another single, followed by yet another sketch, such as a blackface comedy act. The acts that followed these for the rest of the show would vary from musicals, to jugglers, to song and dance singles and end with a final extravaganza—either a musical or a drama—with the full company. These shows would feature such stars as Eubie Blake, a piano player, the famous and magical Harry Houdini and child star, Baby Rose Marie.

In the *New York Tribune*'s article about vaudeville, it is said that, at any given time, vaudeville was employing over twelve-thousand different people throughout its entire industry. Each entertainer would be on the road 42 weeks at a time, while working a particular "circuit," or an individual theatre chain of a major company.

The demise of this form of entertainment took place in the 1930's, with the advent of talking movies and other diversions, not the least being the cheerless, miserable economic Depression started when the stock market crashed in 1929.

The Cyclonic Lady of Vaudeville
Eva Tanguay

The "I Don't Care" Girl, Eva Tanguay

"I Don't Care"
Words by Jean Lenox, Music by Harry O. Sutton
1905

[Vaudeville star Eva Tanguay became closely identified with this rowdy song, which became her personal trademark hit in the early 1900s. It was later performed by Judy Garland in MGM's *In the Good Old Summertime* (1949) and by Mitzi Gaynor (portraying Tanguay) in *The I Don't Care Girl* (1953).

The lyric below is as it appears in the original sheet music, published by Jerome H. Remick & Co. (NY), in 1905. The verses are in common time and are marked "Moderato," while the choruses are in 2/4 time and are marked "Faster." You will notice some of the later choruses do not always fit the beat. Tanguay made up for that with her energetic delivery.

Winners and Losers

Verse 1:
They say I'm crazy, got no sense,
But I don't care.
They may or may not mean offence,
But I don't care;
You see I'm sort of independent,
Of a clever race descendent,
My star is on the ascendant,
That's why I don't care.

Chorus 1: I don't care,
I don't care,
What they may think of me.
I'm happy go lucky,
Men say I am plucky,
So jolly and carefree.
I don't care,
I don't care,
If I do get the mean and stony stare.
If I'm never successful,
It won't be distressful,
'Cos I don't care.

Verse 2:
Some people say I think I'm it,

But I don't care,
They say they don't like me a bit,
But I don't care;
'Cos my good nature effervescing,
Is one, there is no distressing,
My spirit there is no oppressing,
Just 'cos I don't care.

<u>Chorus 2:</u>
I don't care,
I don't care,
If people don't like me,
I'll try to outlive it,
I know I'll forgive it,
And live contentedly.
I don't care,
I don't care,
If people do not try to treat me fair.
There is naught can amaze me,
Dislike cannot daze me,
'Cos I don't care.

<u>Verse 3:</u>
If I call on a friend and she's "not in,"
Why, I don't care,
I simply discover I need some pins,
'Cos I don't care;
Her feeble slight does but amuse me,
Nothing like it could induce me,
To hand it back none could induce me,
Just 'cos I don't care.

<u>Chorus 3:</u>
I don't care,
I don't care,

If she did mean to snub.
I'm feeling so jolly,
'T'would be simple folly
To even feel the rub.
I don't care,
I don't care,
If I do call on her
And she's not there.
If she can't say "Hello,"
She's not a good fellow,
And I don't care.

Verse 4:
They say my hair's in silly style,
But I don't care,
They but amuse me all the while,
"'Cos I don't care;
You see my hair with me's a fixture,
And it's color's not a mixture,
When they call me living picture,
Surely I don't care.

Chorus 4: I don't care,
I don't care,
If my hair is not dressed, swell;
I've got no kick coming,
It's vastly becoming,
And suits my face so well;
I don't care,
I don't care,
I know that style like mine
Is mighty rare.
So no one can "faze" me,
By calling me "Crazy,"
'Cos I don't care.

Ron Chicone

Eva Tanguay, a flaming star that flashed in the firmament for a moment in time, burned brightly and then became nothing more than a dark and charred ember, remembered naught but by those standing on the threshold of eternity.

She entered this world August 1, 1878, in Canada, the fourth child born to Doctor Joseph and Adele Tanguay pronounced "Tang-way." A pint-sized baby that fought for life, she was a mere five pounds at birth, as small as a pin, so she was called the "pin baby," a designation that did not last long. As she matured, she blossomed into a well-constructed young lady with generous lascivious curves she would use to propel her to stardom in the wily world of show business.

In 1883, the Tanguay's moved to Holyoke, Massachusetts. This was brought on because of a massive recession that enveloped both Canada and the United States. Beginning about 1873, it lasted until some rays of light appeared in 1896, more than twenty years, quite a long period of time for a naturally occurring boom and bust cycle to play out. Doctor Tanguay felt that the opportunities for his business were greater in the States than Canada, since Holyoke had the advantage of other members of the Tanguay clan residing there, decidedly a town impacted by immigration from France, the Tanguay's heritage.

The good doctor, apparently was not so good, he debased his life and internal organs with the liberal use of the demon rum. Within three years of the move to Holyoke, he expired and left his family destitute. This, of course, required all the members of the family to work as much as they could. By pulling together, they scratched out a barely livable existence. As for Eva, the precocious one and the only one not contributing to the family coffers, she tended to gravitate to pie-in-the-sky things, such as acting in school, or other theatrical entertainment shows playing locally. What she lacked in talent, she made up with an enthusiasm that was exuded in a rather pitiful, high-pitched voice and frenetic waving of her extremities. Somehow, the audience seemed excited by her indolent ways.

At the age of ten, she was touring in a play called *Little Lord Fauntleroy*, which lasted for two years. Eventually, Eva realized that New York was the place to be to pursue her intended profession. Working from a rented apartment, she became somewhat of a cult figure, attending auditions anywhere, wherever they were being held in and around Broadway.

On one particular afternoon, she made her way down the sidewalks of New York on a rainy, drizzly day in the fall of 1901, carrying a large cloth, lumpy satchel that bumped on her legs as she hurried toward a small theatre. Here she would audition for a nondescript musical called *My Lady* that her agent informed her was taking auditions. However, he did not inform her that they only wanted auditions from those entertainers the talent director had requested.

Her agent was a little desperate finding placement for Eva. She was not paying him in monetary script, because she seemed to be in a continually embarrassing situation when it came to money. Instead, his remuneration consisted of private entertainment from Eva, since she was not above providing services to people who could further her career. Besides, she personally enjoyed it. Her agent enjoyed it too and this was the reason he tried his utmost to get her placed. He did not want his arrangement with her to end.

Turning down a small alley, where, hopefully, the stage door was located, Eva, now thoroughly drenched, trudged to that small entryway in water almost ankle-deep. A single door appeared with a small light above it. Banging on the door incessantly finally brought a response. A small-wizened old man peered out and asked her what she wanted.

"Goddammit, I want in, that's what the fuck I want," Eva shot back.

A little surprised at this assault, he stepped back, and she made her entrance. Mad as a wet hen, she looked at the old guy brazenly.

"Point me to where the hell the auditions are going on," she said.

This he did and she, in shoes that squished when she walked, continued to a small, musty auditorium.

A thin frail man was standing by the stage. Eva approached him and tapped his shoulder from behind. He turned to face her.

"What the hell do you want?" he inquired.

"What the hell do you think I want?" Eva, no shrinking violet, replied. "I want a goddam audition."

He responded in a manner that was decidedly hostile. "Well you are in the wrong place. I'm conducting auditions only for those specifically invited by me, and not for every bimbo that comes along and thinks she can dance."

Her spirits hit the bottom rung and she thought to herself, *I'm so tired of this merry-go-around and now I run into this dolt. When I get back to that four-flushing agent, I will inform him it's the last piece of ass he's going to get from me. Well, I've got nothing to lose, so here goes.* "Listen to me you idiot, I'm probably the best dancer and vocalist in this entire country. I've been on the road for the last several years, and because you won't take five goddam minutes to watch the best thing you have ever seen, you will pass up something you will regret for the rest of your life."

"Oh, for crissake, I've heard it all now."

"Listen to me you jerk. Just let me get changed into my outfit and I will show you curves that you may not have seen before."

This talent director, faced with a brazenness he was totally unprepared for, thought about it for a long moment. "All right, young lady, get changed and let me see your stuff. What kind of music do you want to dance to?"

"Anything that's up-tempo and upbeat."

When Eva returned to the stage and started her audition, she gave it everything she had, which included frenzied arm waving and wild dancing. When she sang, it was more screaming than anything else.

The director could not believe what he was witnessing. In fact, he could not think of an adjective to describe it. His first impulse was to throw her out of the place, but, the more he watched, the more fascinated he became. There was something about the whole thing that drew him in. He thought *what the hell, if I could be mesmerized by this performance, maybe the audience would be too.* He decided to find a small part for her in the chorus.

This then, was the beginning of a fabulous career in vaudeville and eventually in the Ziegfeld Follies. Eva became famed for her rendition of a song entitled, "I Don't Care." Other suggestive songs included, **"It's All Been Done Before, but Not the Way I Do It," "Go As Far As You Like," "That's Why They Call Me Tobasco" and "I Want Someone to Go Wild with Me."** Her style was tailored around her audience and to the era and generation that attended the performances. During World War I, she would sing patriotic tunes and wear military uniforms. Many times, she would do up to three skits in an afternoon, with different attire for each one and then do it all over again in the evening.

To look at Eva, was like looking at a personification of a pert teenager. Her round face, turned up nose, and her blue eyes, looking a little too large, gave her an enduring look of surprise. At the end of her performances she would stop and look at the audience, and in her jaunty, vivacious way with her heart in it, say, "Goodbye, everybody. I love you." And the audience, in turn, loved her.

Her real zeal centered on selling sex, show as much skin as you could get away with, and in her dialog and songs use double entendre delivered in a rapid-style fashion. She brought a new freshness and raw sexuality to everything she did and her connection to the audience was unequalled.

In her day, a new stage show evolved, created by an impresario by the name of Tony Pastor, called Genteel Vaudeville. Tony tried to do away with the last vestiges of the Wild West shows that featured women who held very little back and used language more suited to the frontier. He lectured the performers never to use words that would have a negative influence on children, or on moralistic attendees of such programs. He wanted his shows to attract families, and in this endeavor, he was successful.

When it came to Eva, she would mostly ignore his dictums, but, in some circumstances, she would modify her utterances, ever mindful of the "blue envelopes" delivered to performers informing them that their services were no longer required. This happened when they were bold enough to ignore Tony Pastor's instructions, to their everlasting regret. The color "blue" has since become the loose term for anything, or any form of speech, considered off-color. In other words, "swearing a blue streak" was not acceptable.

Of course, Eva built her entire montage around being suggestive, so, if they wanted her in the show, along with sold out performances, they would have to acquiesce to some amount of ribald and humorous witticisms. Because of her great drawing power, she was able to do pretty much as she wanted. Imagination flowed from her kinetic mind like water over Niagara Falls and her costumes reflected creativity and resourcefulness far removed from the rest of her peers.

In the year 1909, new pennies were introduced and Eva, with a Zen like intuition, created a costume made entirely out of the new pennies. This, in and of itself was a great innovation, but she brought down the house when, one by one, she peeled them off and threw them into the audience, in effect creating a strip tease. She followed that up with a costume made up entirely of dollar bills and did the same act. She finally had a suit made out of coral that weighed forty-five pounds and cost $2000. I don't believe she threw any of it to the audience.

Eva's costumes were not the only things where she was a little off-color. Her personnel life was chaotic and rivaled her costumes. Sexuality was a part of everything she did, and many times, she was caught in compromising situations, which only served to further the reputation she tried to cultivate and enhanced her rowdy characterization in the newspapers.

One notable instance occurred with publicity journalist, Carl Florian Zittel, whose employment was with the *New York Journal*. Widely known as Zit, he served as Eva's unintentional public promotional agent. While he and Eva were enjoying a recreational repast at the Riccadonna Hotel in Brighton Beach, Brooklyn, Zit's wife, Martha, was tipped off and she hired two detectives and her brother to dress as bellhops and enter the room where the two paramours were playing under the pretext of delivering ice water. This little drama was given wide dissemination to the media, and immediately, the prices for tickets to Eva's performances increased. Zit, as a result of the aforementioned incident, gave another kind of command performance in court, answering to his wife's alienation of affection suit. One can only surmise how much of a part Eva played in the final result of that affair.

The "sex-capades" that Eva engaged in were varied and many did not end on a pleasant note. Her choices in men did not indicate a great amount of intellect or forethought on her part. One teenage, amorous adventure had left her in a family way and the experience would mentally torture her for the rest of her life. She carried the baby to term, and because of possible negative ramifications to her career, she arranged for her sister to adopt the little girl, named Florence. To the end of her life, she never acknowledged that she was the little girl's mother, however she did provide money, gifts, a measure of distant love, and whatever guidance she was capable of giving.

Tom Ford was a wooden-shoe dancer who was nothing more than a hiccup on the vaudeville bill and something to be endured until the really interesting acts made their appearances, he eventually morphed into an acceptable dancer, and with a flair for exaggeration and self-promotion billed himself as the world's greatest dancer. Eva was attracted to this loudmouth, because of his titillating ways and his ability to produce sexual excitement in a sexual creature such as her. It certainly wasn't his good looks, for, in his acts he would use buffoonery with his wide mouth and ears that protruded a little too much, which gave him a comical appearance that enhanced his ability to act as a jester.

Tom tried to do whatever he could to entice Eva to marry him. Finally, one evening in Ann Arbor, Michigan, in the fall of 1913, after their last performance, he seemingly caught her in a very subdued and submissive mood, and to her everlasting regret; she agreed to marry the unscrupulous money-grabbing jerk. He turned out to be an unrepentant drunk, living in her world and feeding off the earnings and reflected glory that Eva generated. She even went so far as to include him in her act as a duo.

As time went on, his drinking became unbearable and finally degenerated into abusiveness. This trip into hell for Eva unbelievably lasted four years. One evening, after Eva finished the last performance, she arrived home to find Tom well liquored up. With a surprising wellspring of anger suddenly engulfing her, Eva fired off the words that she desperately needed to say.

"You goddam, drunken sot. I have had enough of your filthy habits and I will take no more. For crissake, take a look in the mirror and see what you have become. You need a shave, snot is running out of your nose, and you can hardly stand up."

"Just a minute you whore, you're no prize package yourself," he sneered. You think I don't know you been runnin' around every chance you get behind my back?"

"Why, you dumb bastard, I have never run around on you, and even if I did, you'd be too drunk to know it. Get your things and get the hell out of this house, *now*."

This last blast from Eva kind of sobered Tom up a little. He realized he was on the verge of losing his meal ticket. "Look baby maybe we're getting a little too riled up and need to think about this."

"Getting riled up, my ass! Eva replied with a great deal of agitation. "I have thought about it and it's time you got the hell out of here."

"It's not that easy baby. I have been helping your career for the last couple of years, and you owe me."

"My God, that is as far from the truth as it is possible to get. You have literally cost me thousands of dollars, because of all the times we have had to cancel shows when you were too plastered to perform. It seems that every time I turn around you need money to throw it away on your pals or all-night poker games."

"Listen to me, baby. Whatever I did was for you and me and I'm not going out of here tonight without any money, do you understand me?"

"Oh, I understand you all too well. It's the same old story. Any time you have opened your mouth it was all about money and 'gimme, gimme, gimme.' Well not this time, buster. You'll never see another penny."

"Yeah, well it's not that easy, baby; a judge may see it differently.

Eventually, Eva did have to confer a settlement on this sorry individual, but she was ultimately glad to be rid of him.

Trials and tribulations for her seemed continually to come in the form of men. She was a tough fighter in her relationships with other performers and had many daunting encounters with other entertainers, directors, producers, and owners of theatres, but that side of her would be absent when it came to love affairs. One notable incident exposed her naiveté and it came in the form of a gentleman who, after a Tanguay performance, sent an elegant note to Eva's dressing room requesting that she join him for dinner. Eva was so impressed with the classiness of the note that she impulsively accepted and had dinner with this stranger. He turned out to be good-looking and impeccably dressed, seemingly a gentleman in every way, with manners that seemed a little too formal. She immediately started a fiery affair that once again, ended in disaster. This impeccable gentleman turned out to be a conman, who eventually drained much money from a very gullible and needy Eva. He went to an extreme that she had never before experienced in her life. ***He stole her expensive jewels.***

Although he was convicted of a felony and was incarcerated, it points out the fact that Eva wanted and needed to be loved. Her genius and success in her professional life did not carry over into her personal life, however. She looked for love in all the wrong places.

Ziegfeld Follies

Florenz Ziegfeld

A new chapter in Eva's life unexpectedly opened in July of 1907, when Florenz Ziegfeld Jr., a dapper dandy, had the premier of his follies on the garden rooftops of the New York and Criterion Theatres, which would eventually become the bully on the block. Ziegfeld was aiming higher than the B. F.

Keith and Albee Palace Vaudeville Circuit. His aim was to garner the best and brightest acts in vaudeville and put them under contract.

Of course, the problem was how an upstart like Ziegfeld could capture the hearts and minds of the theatergoers who regularly attended vaudeville performances. He saw them for exactly what they were, just performances. What he intended to deliver were to be extravaganzas unequaled in the history of show business. This new type of musical spectacular would have, at its base, a bevy of the most gorgeous chorus girls he could find, poured into the briefest costumes it was possible to get away with and hope for the best when dealing with the local constabulary, not to mention an open hand from the local officials that could most assuredly be filled.

The entertainment of choice would be the best dancers, singers, and musicians that money could entice. And entice he did, using prodigious amounts of it to offer the best performers on the vaudeville circuit and other venues more money. This was his calling card and who among them would not listen to the clarion call of more dollars?

His chorus girls danced to choreographed works of prominent composers, such as Irving Berlin, George Gershwin, and Jerome Kern. His Follies featured many performers who, though well-known from previous work in other theatrical genres, achieved unique financial success and publicity with Ziegfeld. Included among these were Nora Bayes, Fanny Brice, Ruth Etting, W. C. Fields, Eddie Cantor, Marilyn Miller, Will Rogers, Bert Williams, and Ann Pennington. Eva was among the stars that he wanted, not only because she could fill seats, but her dialogue was racy, but not blatantly vulgar and she wore very brief costumes that met with his approval.

The 1909 Follies was a dramatic and musical farce as reported by the *New York Dramatic Mirror*. *"This is an example of the attitudes of the moralistic rectitude of a segment of the population at that time."* In actuality, the Follies was a tremendous hit and was embraced by the vast majority, who called it earth-shattering and far and above anything they ever saw in a theatre. It featured rich scenery that changed every fifteen minutes, coupled with a pulchritudinous female chorus of unparalleled proportions. The chorus became the Holy Grail of that show of shows.

Headlining this stunning edition of the Ziegfeld Follies was an entertainer called Nora Bayes. Her act had a good deal of a resemblance to Eva Tanguay's much to her chagrin. Eva had not, as of yet, been approached by Ziegfeld. Behind the scenes, the Follies were not as peaceful as Ziegfeld preferred it to be. The elephant in the room, as it usually is, was money, and of course, it involved the amount of money that Mrs. Bayes felt *she* should be earning. During this period, in 1909, Nora Bayes was earning twelve-hundred dollars a week and felt she was worth more. Her husband, who was also appearing in the show, was earning only two-hundred per week.

While negotiations were taking place with Nora, Ziegfeld took the opportunity to contact Eva, who had plans in the works of going to England, where she would receive the highest remuneration any performer had ever received.

The call from Ziegfeld came before her first performance at the Brighton Beach Music Hall in Brooklyn, N.Y. "Miss Tanguay, I'm glad I was able to reach you this day." Ziegfeld spoke slowly and enunciated his words clearly so there would be no misunderstanding. "There may be an opening in my show and I was wondering if you would have an interest in filling this position.

Eva at first felt a little at a loss for words, until her usual belligerent persona showed up. Suddenly a degree of resentment thrust to the fore.

"Mister Ziegfeld, if I may be so presumptuous, why in hell did you not knock on my door when you were putting together your little show?"

"Miss Tanguay, you are a headliner and I honestly did not think you would be interested in something that no one knew if it would be a hit or not. Besides, money was of the essence and I frankly did not think we could afford you."

"Let me inform you of a bit of news you may not be aware of. I'm currently packing my things for a trip to England. This is to be the first performance of my planned tour of the Continent, put forth by B. F. Keith and E. F. Albee. I have been offered an unbelievable amount of money, the most any American performer has ever been offered."

Ziegfeld became somewhat unsettled, but his temperament was such that it would not allow him to give up easily. "If you would allow me Miss Tanguay, may I invite you to dinner on a night of your choosing to pursue this subject matter to a fuller extent?"

"Mister Ziegfeld, it may be a waste of your time and mine. The amount of money you are prepared to offer would probably be offensive to me. So, rather than it be an affront, I will go my way and you can continue on yours. How did you put it? Go find someone to fill an opening in your show." With that she hung up.

Her impertinence was something Ziegfeld would not be comfortable with and he immediately grabbed his assistant and informed him that they would be working that evening. After her last performance of the evening, as Eva was in the process of getting ready to relax at a club in Brooklyn with other friends from the show, she was informed that two gentlemen wanted to see her.

"Who the hell are they and what do they want?"

"One gentleman said he was Florenz Ziegfeld."

"Oh shit! What is *he* doing here?"

Eva was entertaining the thought, she was about to face an undue amount of invective, slowly descended the stairs to the lobby where he waited, not her usual bubbly self as she ruminated over what his reactions would be. She now felt a little remorse in the way she ended that phone call. After all, he was currently the biggest thing in show business and she was always mindful of future engagements. Eva, even though she was the highest paid performer in show business, had a continuous love affair with money. She spent recklessly, was very generous with her friends and then fought like a tigress for more compensation.

Her pace quickened as she neared the lobby, having formulated in her mind the words she would use to placate Mister Ziegfeld. As they approached each other, Florenz held out his hand, took hers, and in an old world gesture, bowed and lightly kissed the back of it. This gesture, coming from a tall, refined and elegantly mannered man, with his pencil-thin mustache, seemed completely natural. As her hand fell from his, he looked directly into her eyes.

"Miss Tanguay, I cannot express enough how thrilled I am to gaze upon your countenance and behold your outstanding beauty. I am bereft of any arrogance while in the emanations of your aura."

Eva looked away and tried to hold back involuntary schoolgirl giggles. His manner in the way he introduced himself came as a complete surprise to her and she momentarily lost her composure. After an awkward pause, she spoke.

"I am sorry for the way I ended the conversation on the phone. Please accept my apologies. I can be abrupt at times if I feel that there is disrespect when someone speaks to me. Before a show I am completely engrossed in what my stage presence will be and am put-off when I'm interrupted in my meditations."

"Miss Tanguay, please accept my abject apologies. I certainly would never have disturbed you if I had thought that it was an inappropriate time. I assure you, that happenstance will never occur again."

"So, tell me Mister Ziegfeld, what has brought you all the way to Brooklyn? If it is to purchase my services for your show, as I explained over the phone, I'm already spoken for. I'm

Winners and Losers

expected in Merry Old England in a short while and my sponsors will not be accepting of my failure to comply."

"Miss Tanguay, if I may, my traveling to see you this evening was to invite you to dinner and let me give you the spontaneous revelation of the truth. Yes, I very much want you in my show and I am ready to present to you some very attractive terms, which your sponsors would not want you to discard. You, or I, can explain to them the immense value that you would have after touring with the Ziegfeld Follies, and the next time you accept an engagement overseas, the amount you will receive will be enhanced considerably. I beg your understanding, but Mister is not a part of my name; Flo or Zig will be sufficient."

"And Miss is not a part of my name. I don't miss anything unless it's a great love life. Call me Eva."

This last sentence made Florenz do a double take, because he tended to be, let us say, very amorous with the girls in his show. Eventually, together they nailed down the extravagant terms of the contract and Eva thus became a headliner in The Ziegfeld Follies.

Ziegfeld wasted no time in breaking off negotiations with Nora Bayes, which, by this time had become rancorous. Though he ended up paying Eva a greater sum than he had anticipated, it was worth it to him because of what he felt was an injustice done to him by Nora, with her money-grubbing ways.

∞∂∞

Sophie Tucker

As Eva's star rose in the Follies, she became more demanding and iconoclastic. One revealing moment came about when she decided that a song titled *Moving Day in Jungle Town*, which belonged to rising star, Sophie Tucker, should be the one she sang. This act of Eva's had the effect of eliminating Sophie from the show and Sophie was obviously hurt by Eva's childish stunt.

Later, in Eva's declining years, she was losing her eyesight and was, for all intent and purposes, insolvent, Sophie paid for an operation on Eva's eyes, since, in those later years, they had become best friends. This defining moment in a life so richly lived, tells you all you need to know about the character of Sophie Tucker, known as the Last of the Red Hot Mommas.

As the years progressed, Eva succumbed more and more to the ugliness of paranoia and she would not allow anyone to watch her performance from the wings. She went so far as to stab a gentleman in the stomach with a hatpin at one performance, while he was standing in the way as she left the stage. The injured party hauled her into court and sued her. A doctor the court brought in to testify about the injuries, however, just happened to be a friend of Eva's and Eva was found not culpable.

She used this same weapon at a performance with John Philip Souza and his band at an appearance on the same bill at the most elegant theater in America, *The Palace* in New York City. He inadvertently backed into the heavily draped curtain behind Eva as she was performing on stage. It was so slight that no one in the audience could discern the rustling of it, but Eva noticed, and she removed a hatpin from her headpiece and stuck it into the March King's rear-end. He thereupon howled inelegantly in pain, leaving the audience to wonder over the commotion.

Much of the mental struggles Eva had with her psychological condition were brought on by her desire to improve and live up to the accolades she received. Aware of her inadequacies, she was received by the multitudes with acclaim, she knew within herself that she was, at best, a trifling singer and an obviously inadequate dancer, who made up her insufficient talents with explosive enthusiasm, wit, and charm while on stage. Derogatory comments were magnified in her mind and became the devil incarnate, driving her to the brink of insanity, manifested in paranoia and periods of deep anger expressed when she felt those around her formulated expressions of what she took to be disrespectful statements. When this happened, Eva would lash back with scathing and malicious language, yet, through all this, she maintained her unswerving loyalty and generosity to those she thought were her friends.

∞∂∞

Mae West

The story of Eva Tanguay would not be complete without a section on the girl that brought Hollywood and the entertainment industry to its knees and inadvertently started Eva's decline—Mae West. Mae became her bawdy self because of her adulation of the cyclonic and naughty Eva. As a young girl, her youth was spent under the auspices of her mother, who, with prescience, directed this young lady to closely observe every nuance of Eva's stage routine.

She eventually became a star in her own right, even though she never attained the fame that belonged to Eva. In that era, it may have been her more overt, in-your-face sexuality, which did not compare to Eva's subtle, more accepted—at that period of time—sexual connotations. Eventually, Mae began writing her own risqué plays using the pen name, Jane Mast. Her first starring role on Broadway was in a 1926 play, entitled *Sex*, which she wrote, produced, and directed. Although critics panned the show, ticket sales were brisk. The production did not go over well with city officials, however, and the theater was raided, arresting Mae, along with the cast. They were taken to the Jefferson Market Court House (now Jefferson Market Library), where she was prosecuted on morals charges, and on April 19, 1927, sentenced to ten days in jail for "corrupting the morals of youth." While incarcerated on Welfare Island (now known as Roosevelt Island), she dined with the warden and his wife and told reporters that she had worn her silk panties while serving time. She served only eight days, with two days off for good behavior. Media attention surrounding the incident enhanced her career. Later, when asked about censorship, and how it probably ruined her career, she replied, "I thought it was great, I made a fortune off of it."

Once when a hatcheck girl commented on her diamonds, saying, "Goodness those diamonds are beautiful," Mae replied, "Goodness had nothing to do with it, dearie."

The handsome Cary Grant received his first starring role in movies because of Mae. She happened to see him on the movie lot, turned to the director, and told him she wanted that gorgeous guy in her movie. The director pointed out that he was a very inexperienced actor, but Mae said, "If he can talk I'll take him."

Mae and Eva remained friends until Eva's death in 1947 at age 67.

Winners and Losers

The Wall Street Crash, 1929

1929 became a watershed year for Eva. From this point, her career took a downward tilt and could not be righted. Money problems developed into a morass of red ink. Surprisingly, she had managed to build an estate with an asset value of two million dollars, composed of real estate, securities, stocks and bonds.

The stock market started gyrating in an uncharacteristic manner in March of 1929, and at one point, took an unsettling dive, but rallied again in the summer. Unbeknownst to the nation, this portended the crash that occurred later that year, in October. This spelled the horrific end of the Roaring Twenties.

The beginning of the year was benign as far as the securities markets were concerned. The market, as usual, continued on its customary path upward and all seemed right with the world, at least in Eva's world. It had a cogency that gave Eva no cause for concern. She had put a customer's man in charge of her far-flung investments and paid little attention to the way her assets were being invested and why should she? Everything up to then had been going well and The Market was an element that tended to bore her.

On the evening of October 24, called Black Thursday, the market declined eleven percent, heralding the crash five days later, October 29, a day that went down in history as Black Tuesday, Eva, at last, detected something was amiss. She immediately called for her driver, a large burly man she had personally picked for his size and menacing look, and headed for Wall Street, where her brokerage firm was located. As they neared the famed street, it seemed all hell was breaking loose. Traffic came to a complete stop and they were forced to join the massive amount of humanity jamming the streets in helter-skelter fashion. Eva was being shoved and jostled around so much the driver feared for her safety and did his best to shelter her from the wild, shouting crowd.

All around her swirled people who were in fear of losing their money, and all they had in life disappearing into an unbelievable black hole. There was a run on the banks and the crowd was jamming up in front of the entrances, banging on the doors, trying to get what was left of their money. The banks responded to the crush by locking their doors.

Now, Eva was truly fearful. Events were unfolding far too fast for her to comprehend. Nothing made sense to her anymore and she wondered what the hell was going on. Had the whole world gone crazy? She felt like she was in a movie, with the reel on fast forward. The feeling was surreal; no matter how fast she ran, she could not catch up. This was mass hysteria on a level that she had never in her life experienced. Unreasonable fear welled up in her throat, choking her and she could not catch her breath.

She and her driver went on as best they could, desperately trying to reach her broker's offices. They finally arrived at the entrance of his establishment after her driver pushed and pulled her to where a clutch of people were yelling incomprehensible epithets. Through sheer determination and brute force, they entered his building, where the broker found them before they found him.

He approached Eva, and looking extremely harried in a rumpled suit, with profuse beads of sweat on his forehead, took the bull by the horns. "I know why you're here," he said.

"Jesus Christ, please tell me what is going on," Eva gasped, trying to catch her breath.

"We have had a little glitch in the market and it fell more than expected today," he replied, in a manner that he hoped would be reassuring to her, "but, please, don't worry; we think it will be back up tomorrow. I have reliable information that a group of bankers have formed a syndicate and will start a wide-ranging buying program tomorrow. I must tell you, though, that you will have to advance more capital to cover your margin."

"What the fuck are you talking about? I don't know anything about margin, or whatever, and you already have all the money I have in this world. I want you to get something straight; if you don't come up with my money I'll ruin you."

"Eva, if this market doesn't come back tomorrow, you will not have to ruin me; it will already have happened." He dejectedly turned and walked away without looking back.

That was the end of Eva's two million dollars.

∞∂∞

Eva's star faded precipitously in the 1930s, when the entertainment field underwent a wholesale change. Big Bands and movies were all the rage. Mae West tried to do all she could to change with the times and was partially successful. Eva did attempt a movie, but it was a failure. Her type of talent was no longer in vogue.

She was aging and was not able to keep up her frenetic pace of yore. Physical problems were also becoming more and more of a hindrance. The body shape she loved to show off was now turning into a blocky figure, not as pleasant to look at. Her eyesight was deteriorating because of cataracts, as well.

Reduced to taking appearances in smaller theatres for infinitesimal amounts of money compared to what she used to earn, it was now a matter of survival and earning enough just to pay the bills. Her infirmities and the excitement and enthusiasm that marked her former presentations, limited the length of her shows. Her love affairs were now a thing of the past and that was, more than likely, a blessing. Her last marriage, to her accompanist, who was literally half her age was a desperate attempt to resurrect her career. When she realized the publicity over it was not working, she quickly divorced him.

Her last years were spent in Hollywood, California, in a small cottage, a threadbare little place. She used newspapers and old faded pictures to hide the plaster's deformities on the walls. Entertainers she had known and those associated with the entertainment industry came to her aid, visiting her and providing financial assistance. Sophie Tucker, Mae West, Sid Grauman, of Grauman Theatre fame, and numerous others, along with doctors' nurses and caregivers, generously gave of their time and expertise.

Eva Tanguay in her darkest hour, kept thinking she would make a comeback and again be America's foremost darling. Eva passed away January 11, 1947. Her bank account totaled about five hundred dollars, all owed to creditors.

She left an estate of a few minor possessions.

No, she left more than that, she left a legacy of entertainment that still emanates and reverberates from entertainment stars Madonna, and Lady Gaga and other budding personalities.

Winners and Losers

A quote from Wikipedia about Madonna:

"Madonna's use of sexual imagery has benefited her career and crystalized public discourse on sexuality and feminism."

Madonna

Lady Gaga

Does that have a ring of familiarity about it?

Ron Chicone

Ron Chicone

EPILOGUE

While writing this book it occurred to me that the immense effort I put forth may all be for naught. Much of what I have written is predicated on the long ago past. My soul is an old soul that reveres things that transpired before I was born, but never the less those periods have become timeless in my concept of what life is all about.

    Let me return to the big bands, saxophones, trumpets, trombones, clarinets etc. I want to hear Harry James, Glen Miller, Gene Krupa, Guy Lombardo, big bands all. I am still in love with the Foxtrot, Charleston, Jitterbug, and yes the Waltz. All seemingly lost in the crassness of today's dancing.

    I want to perceive and luxuriate in the sound of a symphony with the wonderful violins of a string orchestra.

    Let's go to a dance and glide across the floor instead of standing in one spot jumping up and down in rhythm to the drumbeat out of the Congo. Guitars are okay I guess, but they don't produce the music that emanates from New York's Rainbow Room.

    How about picnics at a small swimming hole where you swing out from a gentle hill on an old tire and drop into the refreshing water and then swim to a raft anchored in the middle of the lake Where good looking gals wearing one-piece bathing suits were luxuriating.

    Does anyone remember getting dressed for church? Getting dressed to ride on an airplane? Playing kick the can under the streetlights? Women in frilly dresses instead of boots and skintight jeans.

    Men were daunting when finishing off their ensemble with a Homburg, a Panama or a straw hat referred to as a Boater. Oooh c'mon you remember what a Homburg was, don't you?

    Picnics on a Sunday afternoon or wiener roasts by a blazing fire in the moonlight? Not to mention, you did not have to go to the Kentucky Derby to see beautiful girls in heart stopping hats. Church would do. Wearing a shirt and tie to Grandma's for Sunday dinner. Conversation at this feast was generally light, uplifting, and hilarious as we bantered with each other and made deprecating remarks with a twinkle in our eye.

All of the beautiful times came to an abrupt shuddering halt when the Second World War started. We looked around the dinner table at Grandma's where the family would gather, and observed the empty chairs, tears would fill our eye's and the twinkle was gone as we realized those chairs would never be occupied again in the same way.

Life resumed again but never with equivalency. Eventually aunts. uncles, and cousins' had families and moved away. Grandma and Grandpa passed on and the tradition of the old Sunday dinner was no longer.

Somewhere a new tradition takes root and life goes on.

This book was in the thinking stage for a decade and the compilation period for over three years. In that time I watched as the passing parade passed me by.

I remember
   I remember
      I remember
         I remember.

Ron Chicone

www.ingramcontent.com/pod-product-compliance
Lightning Source LLC
Chambersburg PA
CBHW071659160426
43195CB00012B/1514